What

Dirk Elliott has put the "Method" back into Methodism as he succinctly shows us how to create new and vibrant ministries in communities where the flame has flickered or been snuffed out! As a student of his for nearly a decade and a Vital Merger pastor who is putting Dirk's method to the test, let me assure you—THIS WORKS! We began a Vital Merger combining members of four congregations using Dirk's approach... and have met or exceeded every one of his "Measures of Success" as we approach year five. This book is a gift to the church of Jesus Christ!

Scott T. Walsh
Lead Pastor
New Leaf United Methodist Church

As denominations work to create more vital congregations, Dirk Elliott shares a new way to bring growth and health to existing congregations through Vital Mergers. This book offers a step-by-step approach to a successful Vital Merger, giving helpful examples of what to do — and what not to do.

I encourage the use of the book for any congregation that is considering doing something new.

Deborah L. Kiesey
Bishop of the Michigan Area
of The United Methodist Church

Dirk's long awaited work on Vital Mergers is both his premarital counseling guide and wedding gift to congregations that have a sense of vision and purpose beyond themselves and for the communities God has called them to serve. This innovative and instructional manual comes right out of Dirk's own leadership, experience and passion for the church that could be if congregations can get serious again about missional movement rather than maintenance.

Gary Shockley
Church Planter and Strategist
Author and Senior Pastor of St. Andrew UMC, Denver, CO

Elliott is one of the true experts in the emerging field of church mergers. He has personally guided many successful mergers in rural, suburban, urban and inner-city contexts utilizing what he calls his "Vital Merger" process. Elliott's book describes the step-by-step process he has created and refined for more than a decade. The Vital Merger approach rejects traditional models and focuses on creating a merged congregation based on a new-church-start paradigm. Elliott's approach represents a "new wine in a new wine skin" approach that has a proven track record of creating healthy, growing congregations.

The book is highly readable and is replete with numerous examples from real church mergers. Those planning to lead a merger will appreciate the appendices which include a Vital Merger checklist and examples of key documents needed for the process. A final section describing the characteristics of Vital Merger planting pastors can help clergy discern whether they are suited for such an undertaking.

Christopher R. Gambill, Ph.D.
Center for Congregational Health
Wake Forest Baptist Medical Center

Churches, especially mainline Protestant congregations, today are all seeking new ways to build vital ministries and faith communities. This book provides a road map to do just that. Grounded in years of experience working with many types of churches, Dirk Elliott offers a visionary guide into how to successfully create a Vital Merger and a new church. If you are interested in building vital churches, this will be one of your 'go to resources.' With stories, examples and sample documents, this book should become required reading for lay leadership, and clergy alike and I highly recommend it to all district superintendents, bishops and others serving in church leadership structures. A must read!

Melanie Carey, District Superintendent
Detroit Renaissance District, Detroit Annual Conference
of The United Methodist Church
Author of *Pentecost Journey*

Dirk Elliott has given us a tried and true model for church mergers. Any church considering merging with another church must read this book.

Bill Easum
21st Century Strategies, Inc.

Vital Merger

Vital Merger *is a must-read for any pastor, congregation, or denominational staff considering the possibility of merging congregations. Dirk Elliott builds on the lessons learned from countless broken and disappointing mergers in the past, to show us strategy that creates a growing, fresh new faith community. Dirk's hand's on experience in this ministry has given us a practical handbook that offers a tried and true path toward vital, fruitful and healthy mergers.*

Bob Crossman
Minister of New Church Starts and Path 1 Strategist
Author *Committed to Christ: Six Steps to a Generous Life*

Dirk Elliott has gifted the church with an essential guide to move congregations considering change from survival to mission-compelled vitality. Vital Mergers offers local churches a chance for a clear pathway to move out of "horse and buggy" historical location into a new partnership commitment to the real demographics of their communities. Using more than a decade of experience in congregational growth and new church starts, Elliott is able to pinpoint stepping stones and name the pitfalls, creating a very practical process for local church leadership, congregational developers and judicatory leaders. This is a much needed tool in the congregational vitality toolbox!

Jerome R. DeVine
Director of Connectional Ministries
Detroit Conference of The United Methodist Church

Dirk Elliott validates another option to add to the church merger possibilities—the Vital Merger. This is a merger where two or more congregations join together in a new location under a new name with a new pastor and a new vision. It is church planting through mergers. This is "new wine in a new wineskin" and I like it! Vital Merger is another great resource to assist the growing church merger trend.

Jim Tomberlin
co-author of *Better Together: Making Church Mergers Work*

A New Church Start Approach that
Joins Church Families Together

Vital Merger

Dirk Elliott

Ordering Information:
Quantity sales. Special discounts are available on quantity purchases by corporations, associations, and others. For details, contact the author at dirk@vitalmerger.com.

Orders by U.S. trade bookstores and wholesalers. Please contact Fun and Done Press: (888) 879-1428 or info@funanddone.com

Printed in the United States of America

Vital Merger: A New Church Start Approach that Joins Church Families Together

ISBN 978-0-9746759-9-2

Christian Leadership, Discipleship

First Edition

Cover and Book Design by Bill Kersey, KerseyGraphics

14 13 12 11 10 / 10 9 8 7 6 5 4 3 2 1

To Tricia,
My spouse, best friend, love of my life,
and partner in ministry.

A special thanks to all the faithful, risk-taking pastors
and lay people who have led Vital Merger projects.
You have taught me so much!

"For whoever wants to save their life will lose it, but whoever
loses their life for me and for the gospel will save it."
Mark 8:35

I WANT TO OFFER A SPECIAL THANKS TO THE PASTORS WITH WHOM I have worked who led healthy Vital Mergers. A special thanks to Chris, Chuck, Darlene, David, Dale, Dogba, Evelyn, Greg, Hoyte, Jeff, Jim, John, Jon, JP, Keith, Kim, Matt, Mike, Paula, Rahim, Roland, Sue, Mary, Scott, Tami, and Zack.

In addition to the pastors, there have been countless lay people on Merger Teams that I have had the privilege to work with in this process. I can't begin to name all of these faithful lay people.

Many thanks to those who read and gave input on the book: Kelly Brown, John Schneider, and Zack Dunlap.

A special thanks to my Administrative Assistants who have worked with me closely in these Vital Mergers: Jenni Dodge and Jessica Browning.

I am grateful to my coaches, Dr. Chris Gambill and Reverend Joan Friesen, who have asked great questions and kept me moving forward on this project, as well as many other areas of ministry.

Many people have been instrumental in teaching me along the way. Thanks for all your training!

I am thankful to the Directors of Connectional Ministries that I have worked under: the late Reverend Doctor Judith Olin, Reverend Paul White, and Reverend Doctor Jerome DeVine.

To friends and colleagues who encouraged me to write this book: Doug Anderson, Tom Butcher, Gary Shockley, and Candace Lewis.

Thanks to Bishop Jonathan Keaton, who paved the way for the first Vital Merger in which I was privileged to work.

Many thanks to Christine Kumar, my editor, and Christie Latona with Fun and Done Press for their insight, encouragement, and direction.

Most of all to my spouse, Tricia, as she has served as my editor, sounding board, critic, and constant encourager. Thank you!!

Foreword

MANY CHURCH MERGERS IN THE LAST TWENTY-FIVE YEARS HAVE not ended up as most churches anticipated or desired. The merged churches expected that joining as one church would make things easier and secure their future. Churches entered into mergers driven by financial pressures – they just couldn't continue on their own. It is difficult for a church to come to that realization and to be willing to give up its autonomy. So, in order to survive, they merged by default.

Now after the merger, in spite of optimistic expectations, the newly merged entity does not naturally grow, but instead begins to decline in size. In fact, within a couple of years most mergers drop in average worship attendance in an amount equal to or exceeding the size of the smaller church before the merger. That was certainly not the intent or hope entering into the merger, but that is the harsh reality of most mergers. They do not deliver what is promised or hoped.

Why is this so? Mergers that are based on financial problems and survival of the institution do not attract new people or help them to come to a vital faith in Jesus Christ. However, there is another way, a healthier way, to accomplish a merger – and that is a Vital Merger. Only Vital Mergers can create vibrant new churches.

This book does an outstanding job of taking the reader on a clear and compelling journey into the world of Vital Mergers. This process differs dramatically from other mergers in several significant ways. Vital Mergers:

- Focus on the Mission ("making disciple of Jesus Christ for the transformation of the world"), not survival;
- Seek to do God's will, not the member's preferences;

- Emphasize the need to reach outward to the community in order to be connected in faith;
- Engage in ministry; not maintain facilities.

The book unfolds practical, proven strategies with key steps to take in order to begin the Vital Merger process. Elliott uses the analogy of courtship and marriage to describe this process, underscoring the importance of the spiritual and relational dynamics involved throughout. It is grounded in twelve key commitments necessary to begin the process, which also clarify what churches will need to let go of: their current buildings, pastors, familiar worship space, current structure and programs and names. Vital Mergers require letting go of the past in order to embrace the new church that God is calling into being.

As each step of the process is clearly defined in sequence, there are many examples, learnings (especially from missteps), and quotes to make each step come alive. At the end of each section are important leader tips and a handy checklist to make sure you have not overlooked something important along the way.

This book is a wonderful roadmap to a new future with God. A Vital Merger results in nothing less than a new church with healthy DNA, with a sharp and consistent focus on the church's mission, compelling vision of a future that connects an increasing number of people as disciples of Jesus Christ for the transformation of the world. All of this is undergirded and bathed in prayer, seeking God's guidance throughout the journey.

So why am I so passionate about this process? Because I have seen how it works, up close and personal. I have engaged one of these new congregations that emerged from a Vital Merger in East Ohio – New Leaf United Methodist Church at Conneaut, OH. I had the privilege of spending exciting, energizing evenings with their pastors and leaders on three occasions and watched how they grew and made a difference in their community. New Leaf is not just a merged church – it is a new church with a new start and a new hope with a new mission for new life in Jesus Christ! I am passionate about Vital Mergers because all the hard work and change is really worth it for the good of the Kingdom.

That is my hope and prayer for every church that uses the process in this book – Amen!

Douglas T. Anderson
Director of Church Development (transitional)
Indiana Annual Conference of the United Methodist Church
co-author of *The Race to Reach Out* with Michael Coyner and
Get Their Name with Bob Farr and Kay Kotan

Table of Contents

Introduction:
What is a Vital Merger?

HOW CAN WE COMBINE RESOURCES AND BE MORE EFFECTIVE IN ministry? When people hear the word "Merger," anxiety rises because it implies uncertain change. Some people view the idea of a merger as a hostile takeover with winners and losers. Still others immediately see issues involving loss of identity. Whether the term is applied to a business or faith community, it involves a fear that an uncomfortable change is coming. After a merger, many things may be different. A business may offer different services or kill a product line. A bank may increase rates, change their hours, and lay people off. In all situations, the people that made decisions may no longer be able to do so. Churches may not meet in the location where they once met. Any kind of merger requires foundational change and on the surface tends to feel impersonal.

Furthermore, there are no guarantees. Some mergers fail miserably, destroying employee loyalty and productivity, revenue, and customer trust. Others flourish and thrive. What makes the difference? The answer often lies in the process used to vision, transition, blend cultures, and form healthy leadership-teams.

In the church, mergers are happening more frequently than before. Warren Bird states, "It (Leadership Network) found that 2% of America's 300,000 Protestant churches have been involved in a merger and that 8% are looking into the possibility of a future merger. While 2% may sound like a small amount, it adds up to 6,000 churches!"[1] The increased interest in mergers (up to 8 percent) indicates a need for a systematic process that can increase the likelihood of merger success. *Vital Merger* seeks to lay out one such process: to assist congregations working through the merger process to create successful, healthy congregations through mergers.

Church mergers take various forms. Traditionally, the most common form has been two or more churches deciding to consolidate their resources by moving into the best facility they already own and retaining only one pastor. These mergers rarely bear the fruitful ministry anticipated by the merging churches. Warren Bird and Jim Tomberlin refer to this model as "ICU" (intensive care unit) mergers: "Two churches that know they're in trouble and try to turn around their critical situation, are more survival driven and often fail"[2]

While there may be occasional exceptions, typically the resulting congregation from this form of merger will eventually lose participation and decrease in attendance to the size of the larger church before the merger. So instead of 1+3=4, you get 1+3+much drama=3. Often, the lack of fruitfulness and growth in traditional mergers stem from their primary motivation: the need to survive rather than the need to further their mission.

Another model is an adoption merger. In an adoption, a strong church adopts a struggling church. The struggling church often becomes a new campus or mission site of the strong, vital church. The struggling church is then revitalized through the infusion of healthy DNA and positive brand awareness in the community. The dynamics of an adoption merger are described by Tomberlin and Bird.[3]

Research of traditional mergers with East Ohio and Detroit Conferences of the United Methodist Church, from 2000 to 2010, reveals that these mergers have not brought the significant growth that the merging churches had anticipated. In East Ohio there were twelve mergers during this decade. Two of those mergers would be considered an adoption, where a larger, healthier church adopted a smaller, struggling church. Typically, where adoptions occur, the merged church continues to grow because it was already a healthy church. This was the case in the two adoptions in East Ohio during that time.

Of the remaining ten mergers, nine never achieved the worship attendance of the combined worship of the merging churches. Seven of the merged churches lost the equivalent of the attendance of the smaller church within one year. After a two-year period, one of the merged churches lost the equivalent of the attendance of the smaller church. After five years, two mergers lost in attendance the number of the smaller church pre-merger.

Traditional mergers in the Detroit regional area of the United Methodist Church showed similar results to those of East Ohio. During the decade, from 2000 to 2010, twenty-one traditional mergers occurred. Eighteen mergers could not maintain the attendance of the combined merged churches pre-merger, and fifteen churches lost the equivalent of the attendance of the smaller church within one year. Three merged churches lost the attendance from the smaller congregation within two to six years.

The remaining three congregations did grow in attendance post-merger. Of these mergers, one became a charismatic congregation shortly after merger and has grown in attendance by approximately 50 percent. Another maintained its pre-merger attendance until year six when it underwent a traditional merger with yet another church, and its attendance plummeted. The third church initially lost 22 percent of its attendance and took six years to achieve its pre-merger numbers. Traditional mergers seldom result in the growth or health of churches.

In response to the poor results of traditional mergers, while addressing the fact that many churches can no longer be viable as a single-church parish, a new model of merger is needed to decrease potential conflict and increase healthy growth. The Vital Merger model was developed over a ten-year period, working with the pastors and lay leaders of several mergers.

Instead of consolidating resources or using an adoption model, the Vital Merger strategy creates a new church—a healthy, growing, new-church-start with a fresh focus on the mission field and new ways of doing ministry. Using a Biblical metaphor, the traditional merger is attempting to pour new wine into old wineskins. The Vital Merger, on the other hand, creates new wine that is poured into a new wineskin. A Vital Merger congregation is a new work. It is a viable new-church-start model.

Vital Merger is a practical handbook that outlines the key elements necessary for a Vital Merger and provides instructions for exploring, beginning, and walking through the Vital Merger process. The advice, examples, and stories are taken from actual churches that have merged—including processes and practices that have and have not worked well. The names of the actual churches and the pastors, whose faith, courage, and hard work have made Vital Mergers new and fruitful churches, have been changed in order to preserve confidentiality. Their stories have informed and infused the process with authentic insight and witness.

Vital Merger comes from years of experience helping churches to work through the Vital Merger process in order to faithfully reach their mission field. It shares some of the wisdom gained from the process as people have come together to do ministry in a new way. As such, it is designed to be useful for:

- Pastors and churches looking for a merger option that will bring new life and vitality to their congregation. *Vital Merger* can be used as a church-wide study for churches exploring the Vital Merger option. It can also be used as a step-by-step guide to assist Merger Teams working through the process.

- Judicatory leaders looking for a new option for starting churches within their judicatory area, as well as a tool to use with churches that are discussing a merger or cooperative parish. *Vital Merger* can provide another option for those churches, an option that is more effective and fruitful.
- Congregational developers, coaches, and consultants desiring new ways to start new churches or bring renewal to existing churches. *Vital Merger* can be a tool to bring new life to congregations through mergers.

Vital Merger is a part of the overall discussion of new church ministry and will hopefully inspire further conversation and research into creating new places for new people by helping more churches become healthy, fruitful and vital congregations in the Kingdom of God. Through the leading of the Holy Spirit, the faithful will continue to develop new ways to reach more people with the message of hope and salvation through the love of Jesus Christ.

Where is the Spirit leading you and your church?

CHAPTER

1

Start with the End in Mind: Committing to a Successful Merger

THE UNITED METHODIST CHURCH AND OTHER DENOMINATIONS have a rich history of establishing churches in almost every community in the United States. It is a history and a work that churches are, and should be, proud of. However, just as the economic downturn has caused community agencies and local schools to cut back and consolidate, local churches have been affected as well, and have been unable to maintain buildings and ministries as they once did. The rising cost of health care, declining membership, and aging of the church are rendering more and more churches no longer viable as single-church parishes. Churches are looking for new ways to engage in ministry. Some churches are considering merging with other churches to lower costs while maintaining adequate staffing and programs. However, merging churches can be a difficult and risky process. Mergers often fail to produce the benefits that were anticipated, such as long-term growth.

Churches connecting and sharing the best of themselves in a Vital Merger is one way for churches today to proactively address challenges and to birth vital and healthy ministry. A Vital Merger minimizes some of the risks and problems that come with traditional mergers as two or more churches create a new church with a new vision, name, location, and ministry.

Merging churches can be a lot like merging families. Imagine that two people decide to get married, each with two children from a previous relationship. Both of them have their own home decorated to meet their own tastes and have customs that reflect their particular heritage. With marriage, this couple will attempt to start a new life together with their children.

Many decisions must be made, including where they will live. To make this decision, they might consider which home is the most adequate, or needs fewer repairs? Which home is more centrally located? Which home is in the best school district? What furniture will be kept? What decorations and mementos will be displayed? Imagine that each home has limited space, only three bedrooms, and no basement. Thus, the blended family will need to share rooms and space. Children who previously enjoyed their own room may now have to share space.

As you can imagine, this scenario is fraught with potential for stress and confrontation. The children may feel that their needs are not addressed and their rights have been trampled. Children who move out of their home can experience a sense of displacement. Children remaining in their home may feel the other children have invaded their space. To complicate things further, turf issues usually impact everyone—not just the children. Each family member had comfortable routines. Once the other family moves in, everything changes. Sleeping, eating, studying, and recreation are disrupted. Scheduling, decorating, and cleanliness issues become matters of conflict.

Fortunately, this new family has a third choice. They could sell both houses and purchase or build a new home better suited for the blended family. Of course, a new home would not solve all the problems inherent in blending a family, but it would eliminate many of the ownership issues.

Churches are like families. Imagine the dynamics and drama of a family of 25 seeking to join a family of 50. When churches merge in order to survive, much time and energy is spent deciding which church building to use for worship, classrooms, and ministry options. Which decorations will be brought from the "other" church? Which staff people will be retained, and who will be let go? Often, the decision comes down to which building is in the best condition, is the most energy efficient, or offers the best parking and location. Traditional mergers can be painful and too often lose a significant number of people in ministry.

Mergers of this type rarely improve church health and growth. Typically within two years of this type of merger, the average worship attendance will be equal to the attendance of the larger church prior to the merger. Therefore, merging churches for the purpose of sustaining life may result in the loss of the smaller church.

Fortunately, churches have another choice. Using the model of Vital Merger, a shared vision for reaching the mission field emerges. Thus, many of the issues that lead to tension and mistrust are avoided. Worshipping in a neutral location minimizes turf issues and promotes an atmosphere of trust and acceptance. In a Vital Merger, two or more congregations can merge with positive energy, be poised to grow, and can effectively reach their mission field. A Vital Merger is a new work, viewing itself as a new church start.

For a Vital Merger to occur, the churches need to be in agreement that they will follow a specific process and not look for shortcuts. Seeking God's will and recommitting themselves to making disciples is at the heart of this process. Like a couple seeking to blend their families, there are upfront commitments that help keep the process in perspective.

Those who lead Vital Mergers make twelve commitments before they go too far down the road:

1. To bathe the merger in prayer. This spiritual discipline is essential for the churches to be synchronized with the movement of God.

2. To reach more people for Christ. Church leaders are motivated by a desire to better reach new people with the love and grace of God. New ministries are designed to reach the new mission field.
3. To view itself as a new church. The merger is not viewed as a revitalization effort, but as the planting of a new church to reach more young people and diverse groups.
4. To unify all ministry around mission through a new vision. The new congregation's focus is clearly on reaching its mission field.
5. To imbed new DNA quickly through new values. Unhealthy DNA is transformed by embracing new values and habits that are aligned with Jesus' teaching.
6. To eliminate turf issues. All existing church buildings are sold and the merged church relocates to a new location. In addition, the new church's name doesn't contain the names of any of the merging churches.
7. To remove majority ruling post-merger. After the merger, there is equal representation and equal decision-making power. No church has a majority voice.
8. To receive a new church-planting pastor. A pastor who has been assessed and trained as a church planter is assigned or appointed to the new church.
9. To worship at a neutral location. Worship is conducted in a neutral location from the day of the official merger.
10. To organize the new structure with a team-based, mission-driven format. Creating nimble, flexible, permission-giving structures that support mission-driven ministry.
11. To make room for guests. New churches are especially guest-friendly because they intentionally design everything with the guest in mind.
12. To provide adequate staffing for growth. The merger of one or more churches yields a different organizational size—one which needs a different type of staffing model than that of any of the churches before the merger.

The more fully these commitments are kept, the greater the chance that the Vital Merger will result in a healthy, growing new church start. While specific steps to be taken are spelled out in detail throughout the book, it is important to understand the commitments that undergird the journey:

1. To Bathe the Merger in Prayer

Of course, prayer should be the center of everything we do in the church. However, taking the giant step of merging existing, and sometimes unhealthy, churches into a new church start requires that the process be bathed in prayer. Leaning on the ingenuity, persistence, skill, or willfulness of any of the pastors or laity will not result in a healthy Vital Merger. Through prayer, people will discern God's direction for their church. Through prayer, people will be empowered by the Spirit of God to create a new church together.

Starting a new church is a spiritual matter. Through prayer, people can intercede for everyone involved in the Vital Merger, praying for the transition process to be one of Christian conversation, unity, and love as people encounter the inevitable hassles and problems that transitions entail.

2. To Reach More People for Christ

For a successful Vital Merger, the end desire should not be to postpone the death of a congregation, to pool resources for ministry, to gain more workers for an aging congregation, or to get a better building. The primary concern and driving force for the merger must be to reach more people for Christ. Jesus gave the Great Commission: "Go and make disciples of all nations, baptizing them in the name of the Father and of the Son and of the Holy Spirit, and teaching them to obey everything I have commanded you. And surely I am with you always, to the very end of the age." (Matthew 28:19-20 NIV) More people coming into a relationship with Christ is the primary motivating factor in a successful

Vital Merger. Helping people grow in their relationship with and commitment to Christ should be the primary focus.

Bird and Tomberlin quote Tom Bandy, "The bottom line is that *leaders never ask the participating congregations to commit to a merger.* They ask faithful Christians to *commit to a large, bolder, Biblical vision.* The merger is only one step in a multi-year plan to expand God's mission through the creation of a new organizational entity."[4]

3. To View Itself as a New Church

As Peter Wagner has written, "The single most effective evangelistic methodology under heaven is planting new churches."[5] By viewing the Vital Merger as a new church, and incorporating techniques and approaches used in starting new churches, the Vital Merger will be effective in reaching unchurched people.

Think About It

Because the Vital Merger is seen as a new church start, people have the freedom, excitement, and energy to begin anew with creative ministries that will effectively reach the mission field and bring new people to Christ.

The pastor, as well as the lay leadership, must remind people often that their new church is, in fact, a NEW church. Maintaining this view is probably one of the most difficult aspects for the pastor and the leadership team of a Vital Merger. Some people will struggle to see the merged church as a new church, and will try to fit the new church into patterns consistent with their previous church experiences. They may try to adopt traditions that make sense to the "churched" crowd they know and understand. They may struggle to understand and to keep in mind that the "unchurched" people may have needs and preferences that differ from their own. Maintaining the focus and vision of the Vital Merger as a new church with a new vision is critical to the success of the Vital Merger.

4. To Unify all Ministry around Mission through a New Vision

In a Vital Merger, it is crucial that a new vision be established for the new church, and that members from the merging churches unify around this new vision rather than pressing the new church to inherit old priorities and programs. Beware of shortsighted visions such as "completing the Vital Merger" or, "building the new building." If there is no real long-term vision for the new church, the church often struggles after the merger.

As the writer of Proverbs says, "Where there is no vision, the people perish" (Proverbs 29:18). Without a clear vision, the Vital Merger will not reach new people, nor will it fulfill its potential as a healthy new church. The newly merged church must ask the challenging question, "What is God calling us to be at this time, in this place?" As the authors of *Healthy Church DNA* write, "Every congregation must carefully discern its mission and vision, assess the core genes and unique gifts God has given the congregation, and, working from its strengths, develop the skills and competencies necessary to carry out its calling."[6]

Think About It

The Vital Merger process is an opportunity for re-evaluating programs. Over time, programs may outlive their usefulness and effectiveness. With the merger, each program or ministry is evaluated in light of the new purpose statement and vision of the new church.

5. To Imbed New DNA Quickly through New Values

"DNA is a nucleic acid containing the genetic instructions used in the development and functioning of all known living organisms."[7] In life, a person's DNA determines, to an extent, what they will do and who they will become. Like a living organism, each church contains DNA that provides instructions for development and functioning, helping them to become who God has called them to be.

A new baby is born with a new DNA. It is the combination of the DNA of the parents, yet the child's DNA is unique. The members of all the churches involved in a Vital Merger have the DNA of their previous church. With the birth of a new church, not only is there a new combination of old DNA, but also new DNA from the new planting pastor who introduces new values and a new vision. Seeing the Vital Merger as a new church allows people to adopt and imbed new, healthy DNA and values that are more in line with our divine heritage than with our human preferences. Tom Bandy outlines why this is necessary:

All successful church mergers depend on awakening the experience of Christ in the hearts of at least 20% of the members of each church. Those 20% will have the credibility to lead another 60% into the merger. The remaining 20% can and should be left behind, no matter how much they give.[8]

6. To Eliminate Turf Issues

Elimination of turf issues allows for an equal voice for each church involved in the merger. Like the blended family that moves into a new home rather than moving into one of their existing homes, a merged church needs to relocate and rename itself to eliminate turf issues.

Physical place contributes to a church's sense of identity. Programs, traditions, mission outreaches, Vacation Bible school, parsonages, Swiss steak dinners, and even church kitchens all contribute to the identity of a church. For many, giving up their building is giving up their "church" as well as their sense of spirituality.

For the new church to come together in unity, the church must shift its allegiance from tangible buildings and names to the new vision. From this vision, a new location and name emerges that can unify people.

7. To Remove Majority Ruling Post-merger

In order to maintain a sense of unity, no church should have a majority voice after the merger. Important for the Vital Merger's success is eliminating any factors that give control to any single church and creating neutrality in every area possible. Some people reason that leadership positions in the new church should be based on a percentage that corresponds to the percentages of attendance from each church. For example, if their church makes up sixty percent of the total attendance of the merged church, they should control sixty percent of the leadership positions and votes. Resist this notion! There should be equal distribution of the leadership positions among the churches involved in the merger so that the new ministry evolves instead of perpetuating more of the old.

This often becomes a point of contention if one of the churches is larger than the others. If a larger church is growing, has healthy DNA, and has a great reputation in the community, perhaps the adoption model should be considered.

8. To Receive a New Church-planting Pastor

Many times, one or more of the pastors leading their church through the Vital Merger process is deeply loved and respected—not only by their own church, but by the other churches involved in the merger. The church may desire and request this pastor to stay and continue to lead the new, merged church. However, it is rare that the leader who shepherds churches through the merger process will be able to also successfully lead the newly merged church into its new mission.

Some may think it unfair that Moses tirelessly led the Israelites through the wilderness for forty years, but in the end was only allowed to stand on the mountain and look into the Promised Land. It took Joshua, a new leader with different leadership skills, to lead the people across the Jordan and into the Promised Land, forming a new nation, overcoming enemies, and thriving in the new land. Likewise, a new pastor who has the call, gifts, and graces of a church planter will lead the Vital Merger into new mission and life together.

9. To Worship at a Neutral Location

Worshipping in a neutral location is difficult—yet important—to a successful merger. It is a fact: church people like to worship in a church building. They may reason that they should not spend money renting a neutral location when they have two or more church buildings they can use rent-free. Good arguments can be made to stay in one of the existing buildings: save the rent, hold meetings in one home, etc. However, having a neutral site reduces turf issues and helps people stay focused on the vision of the Vital Merger.

If the merged church uses one of the existing buildings, it will stunt the growth of the new church, leaving some people to resent the fact that they sacrificed their church building to become part of the new church. Some may conclude that they have simply joined with the dominant church rather than being part of a new church start. This concept is developed more thoroughly in Chapter 12.

10. To Organize the New Structure with a Team-based, Mission-driven Format

Many churches considering a merger have maintained an old, outdated, 1950s business-style organizational structure known as Functional Approach to Management. Often their first reaction is to duplicate this style in the Vital Merger. However, merging is a prime time to change the course and establish a new structure—one that is leaner and more responsive to the needs of the congregation and community.

Many Church Boards are structured around a majority-rules format that may be permission withholding. The board must be convinced that a proposal is acceptable and risk-free before they will vote for approval. They often want to refer an idea back to a committee for further study. The result is that it slows implementing new ideas and discourages innovation and new ministries. In addition, this form of structure requires that every decision a team or committee makes be brought before the Board for approval.

In the newly merged church, the Board can adopt a mission-focused structure and process. If a ministry or idea will fulfill the mission of the church, if there are at least two people who will lead the new ministry, and if the money is already in the budget or can be raised outside of the budget (and it is not illegal or immoral), the new ministry gets an automatic "yes" vote. Teams given responsibility for an area have permission to do the ministry of that area without going to the church board for approval. As Doug Anderson, Director of Church Development for the Indiana Conference of the UMC, says, "Doers Decide!"

Leader Tip

Leadership, leadership, leadership! Leadership is important in all aspects of church life. Effective leadership is absolutely necessary for a Vital Merger's success.

Just as newly engaged couples do well to honor each other's gifts and skills as they share leadership responsibilities, churches in the early stages of a Vital Merger must decide on lay and clergy leadership roles during the merger process. Who should take the main role in leading the process? Should the laity be in charge? After all, it is their church. They were present before the pastor came and will be there after he or she is gone. Should the clergy lead? Clergy are called as leaders and should lead the church. Why shouldn't clergy lead this process?

Without strong, capable lay and clergy leadership, the Vital Merger will never happen, or it may drift toward the impotence of a traditional merger. It takes strong leadership to say:

We must sell the building.

We must worship in a neutral location.

We must have a new leadership structure.

We must discontinue some of our old programs and initiate new programs.

We are a new church!

11. To Make Room for Guests

While longtime existing churches tend to rely on their regulars and an occasional visitor to get involved, the new church is constantly making room for guests to attend.

The new church must practice radical hospitality. Friendly greeters should be located in the parking lot and at every entrance to the building. Great quality coffee, juice, and water, as well as good, healthy (and even some unhealthy) snacks should be provided and easily located. Undercover hosts or greeters should be stationed throughout the worship area. A guest services table should be one of the first things the guests notice when they arrive in the building. This table should be staffed with extroverted people who easily engage in conversation, as well as help guests locate needed areas such as the nursery, worship center, and restrooms. Small group leaders should be on the lookout for guests to invite to their group. Outreach activities are designed with guests in mind. As people are leaving, greeters should bid them goodbye.

12. To Provide Adequate Staffing for Growth

In most cases, the churches that are merging are small churches and operate like small churches. Normally, they have one pastor who takes care of all the pastoral work in the congregation including leading, teaching, preaching, planning, caring, visiting, counseling, as well as many other tasks.

When the Vital Merger occurs, the church is no longer a small church. Previous attendance may have been sixty, but with the merger of multiple churches, the attendance may be closer to two hundred, or as much as five hundred. This is no longer a small church. Yet, the mindset of many of the people remains unchanged. Foresight must be used to staff the new church adequately for the new size of congregation. Providing staff to meet the needs of this new congregation helps the new church grow.

While one pastor might have been enough for the church prior to the merger, there may be a need for multiple staff persons who serve as specialists in various areas after the merger. The Lead Pastor should be free to cast the vision of the new church, plan for the future, assist the building teams, and preach. There may be a need for a Pastor of Congregational Care who will help those who are struggling with the transition and oversee the care of the congregation. Additional staff in the area of children, youth, or worship arts may be needed. The new congregation should be receptive to the staffing needs of their new, larger congregation.

When these twelve commitments are followed during the Vital Merger process, the new church will thrive. The more thoroughly they are followed, the more successful the Vital Merger will be in creating a vital, healthy, growing, mission-focused church that is making disciples for the transformation of the world.

While everyone's journey toward mergers has unique twists and turns, there are some tried and true steps that everyone must take. Leaders who follow the checklist in the Vital Merger process will be able to move ahead while avoiding landmines along the way. Read through Appendix 1 to find steps to help negotiate the differences of the merging process in ways that will minimize stress and grief, while positioning the new church for future growth.

If the commitments haven't scared you off, read on and learn how to lead and participate in a Vital Merger.

CHAPTER
2

Consider if God is Calling You into a Relationship: Prayer and Discernment

AN ILLUSTRATION OFTEN USED IN CHRISTIAN MARRIAGE counseling shows how a couple grows closer together as they individually grow closer to God. The example uses a triangle, with the husband at one point at the base of the triangle, the wife at the other base point, and God at the top point of the triangle. The closer the couple moves toward God, the closer they move toward each other. (See illustration below).

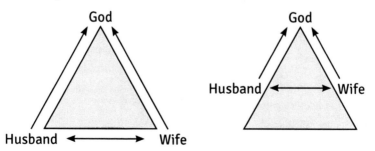

As the couple spends time in prayer and seeks God's guidance for their new relationship, their bond becomes stronger and guides their choices. Likewise, as churches explore a new relationship with each other and seek God's direction, they will grow closer to God and have a clearer understanding of their future together.

Churches exploring the possibility of joining together in ministry must bathe the merger process in prayer. The discipline of prayer is a key commitment to the Vital Merger process. Prayerfully developing an intercessory prayer team for the Vital Merger process, setting prayer as a congregational priority, discerning God's direction, and making prayer the central part of every merger meeting are all necessary for growing in love for God and for each other as well as for coming together in ministry.[9]

Developing an Intercessory Prayer Team

Because a foundation of prayer is absolutely necessary in the Vital Merger process, one of the first steps for the Vital Merger is to gather a dedicated group of people who are gifted in prayer and intercession from the churches in the merger. Some churches choose to start with prayer groups already in existence, others utilize members of the Merger Team, and others choose to start with a separate prayer team dedicated solely to praying for the Vital Merger. Make sure to have an equal number of intercessors from each church saturating the merger process in prayer.

The Prayer Team is kept informed of what the Merger Team is doing and has access to the Merger Team to give them input or share what they believe God is saying to them. Don, pastor of Trinity Church, tells of his experience with the prayer team:

We have a prayer team that has met every Wednesday for an hour to pray. They started praying for the merger and the Merger Team. Now, they continue to meet and pray for our Transition Team and any other things I pass on to them.

Setting Prayer as a Priority

Church leaders should develop a plan that makes prayer a priority in each of the churches considering the Vital Merger. Each church should be listening for God's direction, so they can discern the mission God has for the churches. Terry Teykl, noted author and speaker on prayer, said, "Through prayer, God is able to bless His people and their mission. Without it, spiritual awakening will never come."[10]

An example of setting prayer as a priority was the Fellowship Church Merger where each of the four churches made a commitment to open every meeting with an intentional prayer time. The basic focus of the prayer, according to Pastor Betsy, was for "God to open our hearts and minds to make an impact for future generations. We asked God to have His hand on the process and the future of these churches." At one of the merging churches, the church began a prayer time between the two worship services for people to come and pray around the altar for God's direction. "It was a remarkable time to see God's Spirit sweep over our churches and the community," said Pastor Betsy.

> ## Think About It
>
> Consider constructing a "Prayer Wall" in your new building—modeled after Jerusalem's Western Wall. Encourage people to fill the cracks between the stones with papers containing their prayer concerns.[11]

The Connection Church held weekly prayer meetings with a group of people committed to prayer for the church and for the Vital Merger process. Pastor Carl commented, "We continually referred to the crucial role of prayer in the merger meetings, and each time we hit an obstacle we would table the item until we all had spent significant time in prayer over it. This often resulted in changed perspectives." At each of the worship services, there was a time of focused prayer for the merger. In addition, the church began a small group based on Richard Foster's book, *Prayer: Finding the Heart's True Home.*[12]

Pastor Joe shared how New Life Church kept prayer a priority for the congregations as they merged.

There were many times of focused prayer as we sought to merge the churches, purchase land and move toward construction and relocation. However, the most meaningful is probably our Ebenezer monument[13] in front of our building. At a time of fear and uncertainty, we acquired a couple of hundred bricks. During a Sunday service we asked each family to select a brick and bring it forward, we stacked the bricks as a pillar with a cross on top. At the end of the service the next week, each family took home a brick with the saying from I Sam. 7:12 ("Thus far the Lord has helped us.") We asked them to pray for our church, its leaders and ministry every time they saw the brick, which was to be displayed in a prominent place in their homes. They had the brick for about a year and a half. When we dedicated the new building, they brought the bricks back and we mortared them together in a permanent monument in the front of our building.

The new church came together in unity as they made prayer a priority.

Discerning God's Direction

As the Prayer Team and the churches pray about the Vital Merger, they try to lay aside their personal preferences and attachments so they can discern whether God might be calling their church to join with other churches to create a new church that reaches more people with God's grace and love. As churches join together in prayer and seek God's direction, they may realize that they can be better in ministry by becoming one congregation. Sometimes, churches decide that they are not to merge, but to provide a distinct presence in the community.

For example, in a small rural community, Pastor Carl called representatives from five community churches for prayer every Monday evening. They simply prayed that the Holy Spirit would move in the county, bringing unity in the churches and softening people's hearts to the Gospel message. As that was happening, he also asked leaders to pray more intentionally:

On July 1, I invited the leadership from all five churches to attend a meeting at Friendship Church. The meeting was a short one, by church standards, where I simply proposed the idea of pursuing a merger of our churches and asked each person present to agree to pray for fifteen minutes a day for the month of July about God's desire on the subject. We would meet again at the beginning of August and discuss how God was leading us as His people.

During that month, two surprising things happened. First, one of the churches determined they did not want to be part of a merger. A second church agreed to move forward only if the new church would be non-denominational. The other churches involved were United Methodists, and they would not consider becoming a non-denominational church. As a result, when the churches met again in August, only three of the five churches announced that they would be open to further investigation of the idea of merging our churches.

Carl's passion for prayer, as well as his passion to listen to God and allow God to guide this process, led these five churches in discerning their ministry in the community. Three of the churches discerned together to become a Vital Merger. The people of this new church, called The Connection Church, voted in favor of the merger with over an 80 percent majority.

Another example is The Gathering Church. In the discerning stage of this Vital Merger, members from the five churches involved developed a "Vision Forward Team" to prayerfully discern how God was calling them to:

- Become better stewards of their resources
- Improve relationships between congregations
- Strengthen their joint witness in the community
- Effectively proclaim the Gospel of Jesus Christ
- Reach beyond their church walls.

While an important part of their work was guiding the church through the Vital Merger process, prayer was essential to that work.

By laying a foundation of prayer, merging churches allow the power of the Holy Spirit to move and provide space for God to speak. Paul, pastor of one of the churches that merged to become Journey Church, shared the story of a "God-moment" from one of their Merger Team meetings. He said,

> We most strongly experienced God's leading at a meeting of the Merger Team when we were working on our new mission and vision statement. We struggled for most of two hours, seemingly getting nowhere, when suddenly our mission/vision statement kind of wrote itself. No one person suggested it. We all had something to contribute. We had complete unity with the final statement.

Making Prayer a Central Part of Every Meeting

When the churches that merged to become Fellowship Church began the Vital Merger process, they focused on making prayer a central part of every meeting. The minutes of the first merger meeting state: "We first prayed. Then we agreed we needed to pray, pray, pray, pray, pray!" Bob, one of the lay people at the Fellowship merger, wrote a prayer that the Merger Team prayed at each meeting:

> Dear God,
>
> As we begin our work here today, please help us to remember that we are here for you and that the effort we put forth here today is for you. Please grant us the wisdom to plan a church that will bring disciples to your ministry, members to your church, and will help those in our community who need you.
>
> Please grant us the humility to remember that we are here for you, and provide us the strength to put aside our personal feelings and loyalties so that we may build a church that will last a hundred years; a church that will meet the needs of your children, young and old, in and around our community, the children that you love so much; a church that will assist them in knowing the joy that comes

from accepting and loving you and the eternal life that will come to them when that happens.

In your son Jesus' name we pray. Amen

Leader Tip:

Develop a Prayer Team of three to five people who have the spiritual gift for prayer and who are spiritually mature. The team should meet together on a regular basis. You can also utilize home-bound people who are faithful prayers.

The Prayer Team should focus on the following areas in their prayer time together. They should pray for:

- God's direction in the merger process. If the congregations are going to merge, they must rely on God's guidance.
- All the churches involved in the merger process. Pray for openness to God's guidance and open hearts among the people.
- The Merger Team as they discern the direction, values and vision of the new church.
- The pastor, other leaders, and the congregation's needs during this time of discernment.
- The community needs. Be specific, including conversations and changes happening in the community.
- The new church to seek ways to meet the needs of the community.
- Community leaders. Pray for the leaders by name. Include elected leaders and school officials.
- Receptivity in the community to the new church. Pray that the new church would be seen in a good light and that the neighbors would be excited to experience the new church.
- Unchurched friends of those in the church. Pray for these people by name. Pray for ways to invite them to the church or to share the Gospel message with them.
- The church to have a positive impact in the community to bring about personal, spiritual, and community transformation.

Pastor Betsy, the pastor of one of the churches that became Fellowship Church, said, "This prayer was a uniting force reminding us that the work we were about was God's work—kingdom building work, not a matter of mere money or survival. We asked God to direct us rather than to ask God to bless what we wanted."

When the people of God partner with God in prayer, great things can happen. Jesus said, "I tell you the truth, anyone who believes in me will do the same works I have done, and even greater works, because I am going to be with the Father. You can ask for anything in my name, and I will do it, so that the Son can bring glory to the Father. Yes, ask me for anything in my name, and I will do it!" (John 14:12-14 NLT)

Getting the Congregation to Pray

The Prayer Team should consider ways to include the merging congregations in the ministry of prayer. Expanding the focus of prayer beyond the Prayer Team to include more people in the merger process provides a broader witness of the power of God's presence and of the congregation's need for God's guidance and provision.

A prayer partner ministry provides a broad-based prayer ministry as well as helping form personal relationships among the congregations. Those people willing to pray for the merger process could submit their name to the Prayer Team. They would be paired with someone from another congregation in the merger process to pray for the churches, the merger, and for each other.

Conducting periodic congregational prayer walks in the community is an effective method of including more people in prayer. People from each of the churches would gather and then walk through a neighborhood or targeted area of the community. Before the walk, a member of the Prayer Team would gather the people for prayer then explain that the prayer walk will last thirty minutes. The people may be assigned to different parts of the community. Some may need to drive to the neighborhood in which they will be praying. They are to walk through the neighborhood in pairs or small groups, praying for the people in the houses they pass, and looking for the needs of the community. They should try to see the neighborhood (their mission field) through God's eyes. What does God see when God looks at this neighborhood? What hurts are the people experiencing? A prayer walk is not an extended time of prayer, but a time to be alert to God's presence and the needs of the local community, interceding on behalf of homes, businesses, and neighborhoods.

Men and women who participate in the prayer walk can share their observations with the congregation and discuss what God has shown them. After sharing observations and insights, they pray together as a group, asking the Holy Spirit to guide them as they continue to pray for their neighborhood. Their insights are conveyed to the Merger Team as the team continues to discern God's direction for the churches and the merger.[14]

Another way to get the churches involved in praying for the merger is through fasting. Fasting is the spiritual practice of refraining from food or drink for a spiritual purpose. While fasting, a person is drawn closer to God through prayer and reflection. Not only does physical hunger serve as a reminder of spiritual needs, it also helps people identify with the suffering of Christ and those suffering in the larger community. Therefore, fasting increases the churches' compassion and desire to reach out in effective ministry.

The Prayer Team and the entire Merger Team should engage in a shared experience of fasting. The Daniel Fast[15] is an effective form of fasting for a Leadership Team. Members of all the churches should be invited to join the shared fast.

Another program for fasting focuses on set fast days, such as members fasting every Thursday as they focus on a particular need concerning the Vital Merger. Each Sunday, members of all the churches would receive a bookmark-sized handout explaining the prayer focus for the week, suggested prayer practices, and a list of specific prayer concerns.

As Tom, the pastor of Fellowship Church says, "I believe that prayer makes or breaks the Vital Merger process. I think we can make mistakes, but because of our prayer God redeems and blesses. We haven't tried ministry without prayer, and we don't plan on it."

Successful Vital Merger Checklist[16]

☐ Establish a prayer team with representatives from each church.

☐ Saturate the entire merger process in prayer and seek God's direction as everyone moves forward.

3

Explore and Plan for the Future: The Merger Team

SINGLES THAT HAVE CHILDREN LIVING AT HOME HAVE A LOT TO consider when they decide whether the person they are dating is "the one." They will want to provide a positive transition for themselves and their children as they begin exploring the possibilities and potential problems of married life as a blended family.

Both lay and clergy leaders in local churches also have a lot to consider when they begin exploring the possibility of merging. The idea of the merger often comes from shared experiences with members of other local churches, such as community worship services, local food banks, and other outreach events. From these shared experiences, some people begin to entertain the possibility of their churches merging, and they begin initiating conversations with members of other churches. The Vital Merger process provides a way for church members who are considering a merger to explore and perhaps begin planning a future together.

As churches discern God's direction toward a Vital Merger, the church leadership of all the churches considering the merger should contact the Judicatory official responsible for church planting. The official will preside over an initial meeting with the church leadership to help them understand the Vital Merger process and answer questions. Often, this meeting is held as an informational meeting open to the members. An open meeting expresses transparency to the congregations regarding the merger process.

In the weeks following this meeting, leadership teams from each church decide by vote whether their church will be involved in the merger discussions. Following affirmative votes, each church selects an agreed upon number of leaders to serve on the Merger Team. Often this number is three to five leaders from each church. Care should be taken that the Merger Team does not become too large to function efficiently.

Like dating couples who consider blending their families, church leaders who are considering a Vital Merger will want to provide a positive transition. To do so, a Vital Merger Team begins exploring the possibility of a merger and what planning, preparation, and communication will be needed for the Vital Merger to be successful. The Merger Team should consist of gifted people who are passionate about the Vital Merger. As Jim Collins says in his book, *Good to Great*, "First get the right people on the bus, the wrong people off the bus, and the right people in the right seats – and then figure out where to drive it."[17] These leaders need to be visionaries and strategic thinkers who are respected by others in their congregation, and they must see the vision of what God wants to do in their community through this merger.

The Merger Team is divided into two sub-teams, the Administrative Team and the Vision Team. Each sub-team has specific work that needs to be completed. The teams work in tandem and meet often to keep each other informed of their progress.

Pastor Carl outlines the process they used at The Connection Church:

Shortly after the initial meeting, I developed a plan to address this new work. The lay leadership nominated four people from each church gifted in two areas. The first group of four would be gifted in administration and the practical details of church life. The second group of four would be spiritually mature people of prayer that were able to discern God's vision for the church. The Vision Team's primary task was creating the new DNA for the church. They would listen for God's leading when it came to the vision, mission, and values of the new church.

These teams must not be so large that they are unable to accomplish their work, yet they should be large enough to carefully represent each church. For example, The Connection, which consisted of three churches, had four people representing each church, and therefore had twelve people on the team. Another Vital Merger had seven churches working together and invited only two from each church, one for each sub-team.

The Administrative Team

The Administrative Team works on the details of the merger. They make the decisions concerning the future structure of the church, inventory or contents (such as furniture, equipment, and supplies) from all the churches and how they will be taken care of, financial aspects, staffing, care of current employees, as well as all the legal aspects of the merging and merged church.

The Administrative Team is responsible for laying the foundational structure of the new church. Rather than simply duplicating the structure of any of the merging churches, the team should take a careful look at what structure will best accomplish their mission. The Vital Merger will be a new church and will need a new structure that serves the mission of the newly merged church. Ideally, the structure should be lean with fewer people involved in administrative committees, allowing more people to be involved in actual ministry. The new structure should be team and mission focused, allowing those actually doing the work of ministry to make most ministry decisions.

In the United Methodist Church, the General Conference changed their Book of Discipline (the guidebook defining the polity of the denomination) in 2004 to allow any church to structure itself (within certain parameters) to best accomplish the vision they are called to carry out.[18] This vision-focused approach provides a way for churches to design administrative structures that serve vision and mission. A simple, scaled-down structure of a Finance Team, a Human Resource Team (Staff-Parish Committee), Lay Leadership (Nominating Committee), and a Facilities Team (Trustees) is sufficient for the administrative direction of the church.

The Administrative Team also lists the contents from each of the merging churches and proposes what will be kept and used in the new church and what will be dispersed. This team also decides how this dispersal will take place. Some of the items will be used in the new church, and others, because of duplication, new style of ministry, or architecture will not be needed in the new building.

The Administrative Team is also responsible for the financial matters of the merging and merged churches. They create a new budget or delegate this responsibility to an ad hoc financial taskforce. They oversee the transfer of all endowments to the new church. In addition, they will consolidate all the accounting and bookkeeping systems from the individual churches into one system.

Think About It

The churches that have been involved in Vital Mergers have handled the distribution of unneeded items similarly. Members of the congregations are given an opportunity to purchase any items that are not kept for the church. If a gift has been given to the church "In Memory Of" someone; that family is usually given the first opportunity to receive or purchase the item.

Staffing is one of the most challenging tasks of the Administrative Team. Most of the churches involved in a merger have staff, and often there is great loyalty from each church to their staff. It is not uncommon for each of the churches to have their own paid choir director, worship leader or an accompanist. Most also have at least part-time secretarial and custodial staff. Some churches operate a day care center or pre-school. Many churches have a youth director. Even more challenging, some of the church employees may be members of the church in which they work.

The Administrative Team decides the staffing configuration of the new church. Job descriptions need to be written to define the new positions. The Administrative Team creates guidelines and policies for hiring new employees. They must prayerfully choose which staff members will continue in their positions. Staffing decisions, in particular, have the most potential for creating tension between members of the Administrative Team and the congregations.

The Administrative Team also prepares to sell the church buildings and extra parsonages that will soon belong to the new church. Deeds must be transferred, appraisals completed, and realtors contacted. It is best to use a commercial realtor rather than a realtor who specializes in private homes. Commercial realtors have regional contacts and a better track record of selling church property. Some realtors specialize in selling church buildings. The Administrative Team should be careful concerning boundary issues when choosing a realtor. It is best if the realtor is not a member or a relative of any member of the merging churches.

The final area of responsibility for the Administrative Team is dealing with legal issues. The new church will need to be incorporated. Deeds for all the property must be transferred to the new church. Endowments need to be transferred and cared for in an appropriate manner, being careful to maintain the integrity of the guidelines. The new church must secure an Employer Identification Number (EIN) that is used to identify the church's identity. The EIN number can be obtained by contacting the federal government (1-800-829-0115) and applying for nonprofit status. The church will need a new postal permit number from the United States Postal Service (USPS) as well. United Methodist Churches will need to secure a new church identification number from General Council on Finance and Administration (GCFA). Do not transfer the number from one of the existing churches because all new churches need a different number. The Administrative Team must secure a Group Ruling 501(c)(3) letter for your church, as well as a copy of the 1974 IRS ruling from GCFA.

The team should follow through on legal matters in order to avoid headaches and setbacks after the merger. For example, Fellowship Church hired an attorney to file the proper paperwork to merge the churches into one new incorporated entity. Instead, the attorney created a new corporation and assumed the old entities would naturally cease to exist in the eyes of the state. When Fellowship Church tried to sell their first property, they found that they could not transfer the deeds. Furthermore, they discovered that they were in danger of losing a $500,000 irrevocable trust because proper procedures were not followed. The pastor of Fellowship Church reflects, "At the very beginning of the process, secure a good attorney(s) who is well connected with specialists in the fields of Real Estate, Non-Profit 501(c)(3), and Trusts. They are worth their weight in gold."

Vision Team

The Vision Team is working behind the scenes seeking God for the vision and direction of the new church. The members of the Vision Team must be spiritually mature, strategic thinkers who are committed to the Vital Merger concept and are mission focused. They should be able to identify and put aside their own attachments and work with others to discern God's guidance in this new work. They are sensitive to God's Spirit and are willing to go where the spirit blows.

In the Fellowship merger, the four churches developed a 411 Team, which represented four churches, one vision, and one hope. This group met twice a month to discuss their future and to find common ground. They wrote and re-wrote the parts of the merger document that related to their work (the Mission and Vision of the new church). They communicated their progress and direction to the Administrative Team and congregations.

Pastor Joe of New Life Church took a similar approach where he and six leaders from each church met monthly in a Forward Planning Team. They completed a demographic study of their community from

Leader Tip

The Vital Merger process works most effectively when lay and clergy leadership work together. For example, with the New Life Vital Merger, Pastor Joe said, "We had six leaders from each church plus the two pastors meeting monthly in a Forward Planning Team. The co-chairs from the two churches were the primary spokespersons at the many congregational and joint congregational meetings."

Mergers can be initiated by clergy or lay leadership. In one instance, the pastor who was clearly the major motivator cast the vision repeatedly and brought those who were on board with the vision. On the other hand, in another Vital Merger, the laity of the merging churches took the lead exclusively. They met monthly for more than a year, praying and seeking God's guidance and making decisions about how the Vital Merger would work.

The three pastors, aware of these meetings, pressured those leading the merger meetings until they were finally invited to attend and participate. There was great mistrust of the clergy because in the past, one of the pastors had been assertive in trying to force a merger of two congregations. At the first merger meeting with the clergy, the merger talks were discontinued and everyone left in anger because the pastor of the larger church pushed for proportional control while the other clergy and laity resented and resisted his pressure. Immediately after the meeting, the Chair, who was a strong and capable lay person, called all the lay people who were at the meeting and invited them to another meeting the following week, without the pastors present. The lay leadership "kissed and made up," got the merger back on track, and eventually saw the merger through successfully. The three pastors were moved to lead other churches, and a new, assessed and trained planting pastor helped lead the new church.

the viewpoint of a merged church to understand their new mission field. They hired a consultant who helped them process various issues and conduct listening groups in the church to better understand the needs and desires of the people. This helped the team establish the direction of the new church, as well as assisting in the communication process.

The Vision Team is charged with identifying core values and focusing on the DNA of the new church. They should also begin discerning the Mission and Vision. Leaders of all congregations will be involved in the discernment, but the Vision Team is responsible for keeping this process moving forward.

One of the initial tasks of the Vision Team is to create "Shared Ministry Opportunities" for the churches that are considering a Vital Merger. Often there has been limited interaction among the churches and their members because they do not know each other. They may have different styles of worship, be involved in different kinds of ministry and programs, and even view church differently. The Vision Team is responsible for setting up low-threat opportunities for church members to get to know each other, decide if they can live together as a merged church, and understand how their differences and similarities can help them become a healthy new church. Finding opportunities to serve together is crucial during this stage of the merger, and the Vision Team is the catalyst for this work.

The two teams work separately as well as together to develop the merger document and assist the merger in moving forward. Good communication within and between the Administrative and Vision Teams eases conflict and promotes understanding, which in turn facilitates healthier transitions during the Vital Merger process.

Successful Vital Merger Checklist

- [ ] Contact a judicatory official (if applicable) when prayer team discerns the direction to proceed with a merger.
- [ ] The judicatory official establishes a date for an initial meeting with key leadership from all churches. The judicatory staff person responsible for church planting should be included in this initial meeting.
- [ ] Each church's Council or Board votes to be involved in the merger talks.

- [ ] Establish a Merger Team to discuss merger issues with equal representation from each church. Divide the Merger Team into two sub-teams:
  - An Administrative Team to focus on the logistics and legalities of the merger.
  - A Vision Team to focus on the mission, vision, and programs of the future church.
- [ ] Merger Team completes a demographic study for the existing church communities and for potential relocation sites.
- [ ] Vision Team answers three questions:
  - What is God's vision for our community?
  - How can we best reach more people with God's message of love?
  - What can we do better together than we can do separately?

CHAPTER
4

Group Dating: Families Getting to Know Each Other

WHILE THE MERGER TEAM IS MEETING, THE VISION TEAM WILL BE working to set up opportunities for family members to get to know one another. Casually getting to know each other and discovering similarities and differences is an important step in determining whether the relationship has possibility. People get to know one another by sharing about their work, hobbies, and family life. Stronger ties form as they discover affinities and discuss differences.

Churches need this time of getting to know each other better as part of their discernment process. What are the structures and decision-making processes in each church? What are the theological preferences? What are the traditions that have been imbedded for years or even generations? What are the core values of each church? What are the worship styles? Elements of Sunday worship can be just as sacred to some as memorial gifts and sacred spaces, within the church, are to others.

For a smooth merger transition, the congregations need to spend adequate time dating. It takes more than a couple of dates before people really begin to understand each other and many more before they may be willing to accommodate new ideas and create new practices together. Building new relationships breaks down barriers and helps people value differences that could otherwise become points of contention.

Just as people date before they marry, churches need to build new relationships, break down barriers, and value differences in one another before they merge. The pastors and Vision Team should discover ways to introduce people to each other as quickly as possible. People gifted in the area of hospitality should begin working together to plan "dating" events early in the Vital Merger process.

Think About It

When doing combined services don't forget to consider the logistics of how the offering is collected. A week of lost offerings at any church is a concern. You could color-code the offering envelopes for each church so that each will receive its offering, or you could pass a different offering plate for each of the churches.

Worshipping together on a semi-regular basis is one of the quickest ways of getting to know each other. In two Vital Mergers—Lakeside and Fellowship—the churches of each merger worshipped together on the fourth Sunday of each month. They alternated worshipping in each of the buildings. At the Lakeside merger, the host church's pastor preached. The Fellowship Church merger alternated church buildings, but the host pastor did not preach, and they created a joint choir from all the churches.

The Connection Church rotated worship using all three facilities. The host pastor at each facility did not preach, but invited one of the other pastors to design worship and preach. Some of the mergers worshipped together monthly and others quarterly. One of the mergers worshipped monthly at a local school auditorium. They developed a new worship team to design the worship services, and the pastors took turns preaching at the worship services. Worshipping together gives people an opportunity to fellowship and to get to know one another, and brings them a sense of unity in Christ.

Another way to build relationships in a merger is having small group opportunities for everyone. Longstanding small groups tend to form cliques. Forming new groups and integrating existing groups with new people will discourage cliques and build unity within the new congregation.

In addition, other activities help to bring understanding and unity to the merging congregation. At Living Hope, Mary, the lay leader of one of the merging churches, said, "Choosing a new name early in the process gave focus to the church and helped to blend the two congregations." The two churches that became Living Hope Church hosted social activities, picnics, Bible studies, and fundraising activities to help the people of both churches become acquainted and comfortable with each other.

Pastor Nancy, one of the pastors involved in the Fellowship Church merger, states, "Ten years prior to the merger that became Fellowship, the four churches had been in discussion about joint and vital ministry that could be accomplished if the churches worked together and multiplied their abilities and vision." They developed a weekly, early Sunday morning worship at the lakeshore and brought the youth groups together. Five years later, these same four churches came together and formed the Fellowship Project, reflecting the sense of fellowship they had in working together, a joint ministry of repairing homes for poor and elderly people in their community. Pastor Nancy says:

Our churches worked together on the Fellowship Project which aided the community; our laity took the lead on the project, but as pastors we fully supported the mission by attending monthly planning meetings and working alongside the laity during the week of the actual project. For the first time in many years members from each of the four churches were getting to know each other. We (the pastors) were being looked at as spiritual leaders in the community, not simply in our individual churches. There were no struggles about boundaries or worry that members might start attending the other church. Our laity started talking about how well we worked together and how powerful worship was when we came together in mission. They recognized they could be a strong force for the community and for God.

Pastor Joe of New Life Church created a Lenten devotional guide from stories contributed by longtime participants in the two congregations to assist in the process of getting to know each other, as well as to understand the history of both churches. They also participated in mission trips and local mission projects with members of both churches working side-by-side, creating a sense of unity and common purpose. These joint fellowship experiences were vital in bringing the churches together.

Pastor Joe also organized an out-of-state mission trip for his congregation. The group planned, traveled, worked, served, and ate together. They learned a lot about each other during the trip. Friendships that were formed during that time provided strong glue that helped the congregations merge into a unified community of faith.

The churches that made up New Covenant Church became frustrated by lack of children in Vacation Bible School (VBS). During the dating period, these five churches decided to work together and host a joint VBS. Each church previously had less than twenty children at VBS. Volunteers hosted and held VBS in all five churches, alternating between the five churches, with VBS held one night in each church. This helped them work, lead, teach, and serve the children together. As a result of this joint ministry, VBS was a great success with more than one hundred children present. Volunteers were happy to serve and build relationships with one another.

In another Vital Merger, the congregations chose to forgo their involvement in special ecumenical services during Advent and Lent in favor of doing joint services for the churches involved in the merger. One Vital Merger with seven churches held a joint Ash Wednesday and Holy Thursday Service. They chose to sit together as congregations during the worship service so everyone could identify who was from which church. During fellowship time after the worship, the people were intentional about socializing with each other.

Leader Tip

The question is often asked, how long should the congregations "date" before they move forward in the merger process?

The length of the dating period varies greatly in Vital Mergers. In some churches considering a merger, the people live in the same communities, participate in common school activities, and extended family may be active in several churches. In this community setting, churches do not need a long dating period. They already have a sense of shared values, as well as common community heritage.

Other churches have dated for as long as five years, carefully building congregational agreement and unity, as well as building strong relational ties. The movement toward merger comes much more gradually as the people build relationships and share in each other's lives.

One group of churches discussed merging for thirty years before they began the actual merger process. Early on there was significant opposition in each of the churches. Finally, they were linked together by a judicatory official as a "cooperative parish" and began doing ministry together. Joining the youth group, worshipping together occasionally, and sharing activities helped the people gain the vision of merging.

Although no absolute dating timeline exists, it is typical for most Vital Mergers to have a dating period from eighteen months to two years. During this time, creating opportunities for the people to build solid relationships is crucial to the Vital Merger's success.

In one merger, many of the congregants were campers, so they decided to campout at a state park. These campers from different churches built relationships and friendships during the weekend. They shared meals, played games, went swimming, and told their stories around the campfire. Members who did not camp were invited to visit during the daytime and enjoy the campfires in the evening.

Attending sporting events as a merged church is another "dating" idea that has worked well with some of the Vital Mergers. The church chooses a day to attend a game. They purchase group tickets so they can all sit in the same area. New friendships are formed as they cheer for the home team and experience the excitement of the game. One Vital Merger promoted outdoor events on Sunday afternoons and evenings as a way to build cohesiveness in their new church. During the summer they held several picnics and Ice Cream Socials. They played games, talked, and enjoyed their time together, ending the evening with an outdoor worship service.

The pastors at the Trinity Church Vital Merger hosted a Parsonage Open House with each of the pastors and their families opening their homes to everyone in the three congregations. The pastors lived close to one another, and many of the people attending were able to walk between the homes. More than 200 people attended these open houses within a two-hour period. According to one pastor, the open houses created goodwill among the people as they fellowshipped together. It also helped to build a sense of excitement about the merger.

Since building relationships is important in mergers, some of the Vital Mergers did service projects in their community such as participating in a CROP Walk to raise money for the hungry, building a Habitat House, and hosting a rummage sale. One of the churches had hosted an annual rummage sale for years. As they began discussing the merger, they decided to ask the other two churches to assist in the sale. Members from each church worked side-by-side at the sale setting up, selling items, and packing up at the end of the day. Another merger tried to be intentional about having neutral locations for their initial events, so they held service projects in several off-site locations.

Creating opportunities for affinity groups can also encourage new relationships. Joint youth groups, children's ministries, men's groups, women's groups, and groups centered around hobbies, sports, and other shared interests provide "dating" opportunities. For example, a group for retired men enjoyed lunch and conversation at one Vital Merger.

Affinity groups that serve the shared mission are especially effective points of connection.

Nametags can be useful as people from various churches and visitors are getting to know one another. Creating a pictorial directory also helps people connect names to faces. Each church plans several photo days. Photos are then put in a self-published directory and provided to each family unit in the merging churches.

Utilizing technology can also help people to connect with one another. Developing a "member's only" picture section on each church's website can help people recognize names and faces. A Facebook Fan Page can also be set up for the merged church.

For the Vital Merger to be successful, churches should create as many ways as possible to bring people together to build new relationships. As people become acquainted and hear each other's stories, and as friendships grow, they will be more excited about joining together as a new congregation.

Successful Vital Merger Checklist

☐ Create numerous opportunities for both congregations to get to know each other.
- Organize joint worship experiences, celebration events, and opportunities unrelated to the discussion of the proposed merger.
- Provide a variety of small group opportunities.
- Alternate worshipping sites to become familiar with each other and gain an appreciation for the ministries and setting of each church.

Communication: Building the Foundation of a Healthy Relationship

HEALTHY RELATIONSHIPS DEPEND ON HONEST AND EFFECTIVE communication. Couples form lasting relationships when they are respectful and transparent with each other. If they decide to blend their families, they must communicate effectively and honestly with the children as the families begin the transition to become a single unit. The same is true for Vital Mergers. Pastors and Vital Merger Teams must communicate effectively with one another and with their churches. Honest and effective communication helps leadership teams, pastors, congregations, and judicatory representatives work together to make the Vital Merger process a transition that encourages people to grow in faith and service together.

Use Typical Communication Channels

In most mergers, communication with the congregations is handled through church newsletters, various committee meetings, reports from the pulpit, and well publicized minutes from the Merger Team meetings. The merger is discussed at all the major leadership meetings in the church including the Church Council, Personnel/ Human Resources Team, Finance Team, Education Team, and Trustees/ Facilities Team.

The Fellowship Church merger used a very comprehensive process to keep the congregation informed. They used bulletins, newsletters, pulpit announcements, small group meetings, large group gatherings, Church Council updates, email announcements, information sheets, website pages, PowerPoint presentations, video presentations, newspaper articles, displays on tables and easels, and informal conversations.

The Merger Team should give regular updates to the congregation during the worship service in order to keep them informed and to build momentum toward the merger. For the Journey Church Vital Merger, each of the churches had their two representatives make an announcement at the end of worship on the Sunday immediately after each Merger Team meeting. Another merger offered Mission-Minute information from the laity of each church during the announcements at worship services.

Create New Communication Channels

One merger project developed a web page accessible to members of each of the churches that helped people track the progress. After each meeting, the minutes were posted on the website. PowerPoint and other presentations made to the Merger Team were added to the site. A blog was created so that members and the Merger team could ask questions and voice concerns.

Coordinate and Share the Same Message with All Churches Involved

Like parents taking the time to unify their approach before sharing an important decision involving a beloved child, churches involved in a merger with one another are wise to do the same. Pastor Ethan, one of the pastors of the Fellowship merger, stated, "We held a number of all-church meetings involving the District Superintendent, the Conference Director of Congregational Development, and pastors who had experience with Vital Mergers." Another Merger Team drafted a common statement at the end of each meeting to be released to all congregations, printed in newsletters, and read from the pulpit to keep the congregations informed about the progress.

One Vital Merger presented a multimedia event at each church prior to the merger vote. The members of the Merger Team utilized written information, a PowerPoint presentation, and speakers explaining various parts of the merger process. These methods of communication helped the Merger Team to tie up some loose ends. They were able to get all the information to as many people as possible, including those who had not participated in the other group meetings. The coordinated, up-to-date information helped everyone be informed as they prepared to take the final vote.

Pastor Jason from The Gathering Church explains that they formed "an Information Team in order to keep the members of the five churches informed of all movement and activities of the Vision Forward Team and any sub-teams." He explains that the team performed the following tasks:

Think About It

If you choose to use a digital strategy, don't neglect other channels for those in the congregation who may not have access to the internet or who are very uncomfortable using that medium. Now is not the time to require people to move out of their communication preference comfort zone.

1. Conducted a survey to obtain feedback and concerns from each congregation as it related to the Vision Forward movement.
2. Mailed an initial letter to all church members informing them of the activities and intentions of the Vision Forward team. The mailing included the team's mission statement and a description of the goals and identities of team members and sub-teams.
3. Assembled Vision Forward reference binders for each church, containing the following elements:
   a. Mission statement (of the Vision Forward Team)
   b. Minutes from all meetings
   c. Copy of the all-church survey
   d. Attendance lists from every meeting
   e. Team member listing and contact information
   f. Copy of a letter to all members
   g. Copy of merger guidelines from the 2004 Book of Discipline.[19]

Allow Time and Space for People to Interact with the Information

People need time to process the information they receive, ask clarifying questions, and reflect on their feelings and God's direction for their church. Pastor Jen reported the communication procedure at the Fellowship merger:

> We offered at least two large group informational meetings, inviting everyone who wanted to come from all the congregations. One was held before we set out to begin this journey, and one prior to moving toward the last phase before the vote. Attendance was probably comparable to regular attendance on Sunday mornings.

She explains that later on, after the straw poll, the churches held a 'Town Hall' style meeting in which members of the Merger Team (four members from each church), answered questions, and held an 'open microphone' period.

Address Issues and Challenges with Honesty and Integrity

Effective communication can be a challenge, especially when addressing opposition to the merger. During the process of one merger, some members who were against the merger accused the Merger Team of hiding information and giving partial facts. In truth, the entire unedited copies of the minutes were printed each month in all the church newsletters. The Merger Team offered three town hall type meetings where people from all the congregations were invited to attend a question and answer session.

One example of the need for honest disclosure occurred during a merger of three churches. One of the churches withheld an important piece of information from the other merging congregations—the fact that they had a sizable endowment. By withholding information and holding onto money and the sense of control it provided, this congregation was trying to enter into new ministry with an old mentality that was partially responsible for its present struggle for survival. Effective communication requires that all congregations involved in the Vital Merger be privy to all information needed to make informed decisions. It is better for the truth to be told and the church to vote down the Vital Merger proposal than for statements and promises to be made that are misleading or withdrawn after the merger.

Although communication from and with the laity carries the most weight with church members, clergy support is vital. Verbal support from the pastors helps cast the vision and keeps the process moving forward. Pastor Jen said that the pastors, "met regularly to discuss the process and worked to ensure a common direction and tone to our public and private statements."

At Living Hope Church, pastors Linda and Jacob understood the importance of the merger and worked tirelessly to see it completed. According to Linda, they "gave their blessings and support through guidance and prayer." They spoke about it from the pulpit, communicated information through committee meetings, and answered questions from individual members.

Leader Tip

One leadership issue that may complicate the Vital Merger pro-cess results from a forced Vital Merger where a judicatory official takes a firm leadership role, telling the churches that the merger must happen. In one such merger, instead of two congregations engaging in conversation, forming a Vital Merger Team, receiv-ing an affirmative vote, and then planning together for their Celebration Sunday, a new pastor was assigned as pastor of both churches in order to move them through the merger process. The Vital Merger struggled from the beginning even though the result-ing new church was healthier than its smaller parent churches. Appointing a new pastor too soon did not allow the lay leadership to own the merger process, and the churches missed the healthy transition period of dating, proposal, and engagement.

The ideal Vital Merger has clergy and laity working together and honoring clearly defined roles. The Fellowship Church merger had this healthy balance. The clergy were present at all the meet-ings offering support, encouragement, insight, new ideas, infor-mation, and resources. At the same time, the clergy realized that lay people were gifted and called to lead as well, and the clergy trusted them. The lay leadership made the major decisions, but they often asked the clergy for their insight and wisdom. In all of the town hall meetings or public explanations of the process, the laity led, and clergy provided support by answering questions that were directly addressed to them.

During most mergers, the pastors spend extra time answering ques-tions and discussing the merger with their congregations. At the same time, it is important to empower laity to provide leadership and be the voices of the merger.

One difficulty for a Vital Merger can be truth telling while hon-oring the Vital Merger process. In one of the Vital Mergers, some of the pastors and team members were not completely honest with their churches by not disclosing the entire Vital Merger process, or by shading the facts of it in a way that would make the merger palatable for their congregations. For example, one of the pastors told the congregation that although the merger document stated they would move to a neutral location, moving would not be necessary. He urged the congregation to vote for the merger, then tell the new pastor after he arrived that they were not moving. Although the pastor was in favor of merger, his subversion of the Vital Merger process eventually saddled the new pastor with a church struggling with mistrust and feelings of betrayal. People accused the new pastor of betraying their trust because he was not carrying out what the previous pastor had communicated.

During another Vital Merger process, one of the pastors took a backseat and did not give any verbal support to the merger. He took a let-the-chips-fall-where-they-may attitude. Although he did not openly reject the Vital Merger, he failed to keep his congregation fully informed. Nevertheless, the laity of this church worked persistently for the merger and tried to keep communication open and complete.

In another merger, the pastor opposed it while the congregation was firmly behind the concept. The pastor spoke openly from the pulpit about the danger of "losing the small-church atmosphere" and spoke against the other pastor involved in the merger. The Merger Team, however, spoke often and openly about the benefits of the Vital Merger, and this church approved the merger by an overwhelming majority. Sometimes, a pastor may oppose the merger in order to protect the sheep. Pastors should be encouraged to listen for the leading of the Spirit—sometimes communicated through the will of the people—and go in the direction that is beneficial to the church.

As churches transition during the Vital Merger process to becoming a new ministry together, everyone involved must commit to open, respectful, and honest communication. The pastors and the Merger Team must assure that all information concerning the Vital Merger is clearly articulated so that church members understand what is proposed and can make an informed decision about the future of their church.

Successful Vital Merger Checklist

☐ Establish communication channels and processes to maintain regular communication from the Merger Team to all the churches involved in the merger talks. Communication is best accomplished when the Merger Team communiqué is presented to each church by the representatives from their respective churches.

CHAPTER

6

Straw Poll:
Testing the Waters

PEOPLE EVALUATE THEIR RELATIONSHIPS THROUGHOUT THE DATing life cycle. We ask ourselves, "Does he feel the same way I do? Does she have the same level of commitment I have? Where are the areas that might give us problems down the road? Are we giving or getting mixed signals? Can I spend the rest of my life with this person?"

Churches that are merging need to test and evaluate their new relationship the same way, asking questions such as, "Are people getting to know each other, and if so, can they be in relationship in the same church? How able are they to worship and serve in ministry together? Are the core values compatible enough to join in community together? What would it take to excite them about the vision of our future life together?"

While dating, people rely on conversation and non-verbal signals to determine the course and progression of the relationship. In the Vital Merger process a straw poll provides valuable feedback about the Vital Merger's progression. Periodic, non-binding straw poll votes are helpful in judging the buy-in of the congregation and in pointing out areas

73

where communication may need improvement. There should be at least two straw poll votes during the phase of merger discussions. Pastor Jen of Hope Church highlighted the importance of the straw poll:

> *We only held one straw poll. One of the churches that did well in the final vote did not fare well with the straw poll. This provided us with a good indication of how minds can be changed through the straw poll. I believe this was a good tool as it helped us see a little more clearly where all of the folks (who were not a part of the core group) were in their thinking – positively and negatively.*

One of the Vital Mergers did a variation of a straw poll at the beginning of the process. At a leadership meeting of the four churches, people were asked to stand on different sides of the room to determine their support. They stood on one side of the room if they supported the idea of a Vital Merger and on the other side if they were against it. The sides were fairly even. Half of those present realized that they needed to "do something," while the other half wanted to maintain the status quo. The leaders from these four churches spent ten months exploring their future together and addressing issues and questions provided at that early meeting. At the end of this time, they polled the same group of leaders who were at the earlier meeting and found that all but a few were in favor of the Vital Merger.

The advantages of conducting a straw poll are to gauge support from the congregation and identify their primary objections. The straw poll ballot form should include an opportunity for the people to voice objections and ask questions. The merger team can then work to answer the questions and identify where better communication is needed.

All adults can vote in the straw poll and absentee ballots are accepted. It is good to get the majority of the people to participate in the straw poll so that their concerns and opinions can be heard and addressed.

Even though each Vital Merger is unique, the major issues raised during straw polls are predicable.

Building Issues

Primary concerns usually revolve around land, facilities, and buildings. The people have invested a lot of time and money in their buildings. They want to see their buildings continue to be a place of worship. Many raise questions about the ability to sell their buildings. They often present reasons why their building should not be sold.

Although the sale of buildings is sometimes problematic, church buildings do sell for a variety of purposes. The majority of the buildings are sold to other churches that want new space. Most times, these church buildings are sold outright. However, buildings have been sold on land contract. The land contract worked especially well for one church because the buyer, after paying a significant down payment and remodeling the church facility, eventually gave the property back to the seller. When a church has considerable debt on its building, it might be difficult to buy another building because of credit issues.

One church facility was sold to a creative arts company that used the classrooms for art classes and others spaces for practice and performances. One small church sold its building to a church located on

Building Questions

- Why do we need to sell all of our buildings?
- What will happen to our buildings?
- How can we sell our buildings with the depressed real estate market?
- Who would want to buy our buildings?
- Can we keep one or more of our buildings for mission and outreach work (e.g., a soup kitchen or clothing bank)?
- Why would we build a new facility instead of using an existing one?
- Where will we meet in the interim from the time of the merger to the completion of the new building?
- How will our legacy be remembered?
- Why would we want to sell to other churches or the "competition"?
- What will happen to all of our stuff?

adjacent property, and that church demolished the building for additional parking. One facility was sold to the city government for additional office space and city council meetings, and another was sold to a school that used the space for administrative purposes such as school board meetings. At the time of this writing, the real estate market is slow, and some buildings have taken up to two years to sell. Churches fare better when they contact a commercial realtor who is experienced in selling church property.

Some people ask, "Why would we want to sell our church buildings to the 'competition'?" The Vital Merger process is a good opportunity to reframe views of "the competition" and recognize that we are all a part of God's Kingdom. Once, the disciples came to Jesus complaining that some who were not a part of their group were preaching, healing, and casting out demons. Jesus said that those who are not against you are for you.[20] Vital Mergers expand the work of God even further when working with other churches and helping them to better utilize church buildings.

Many ask why they need to move into a new facility. A successful Vital Merger creates neutral space and eliminates ownership issues. Moving to a new facility creates joint ownership and offers a sense of belonging for everyone in the new congregation. Many older church buildings feel and smell old, are expensive to maintain, and are usually not conducive to twenty-first century worship. (This issue is addressed more fully in Chapter 12).

If the merged church desires to build a new building, questions arise around where they will meet in the interim. People ask why they cannot remain in their own facilities (which are rent-free) until they get the new building built, or at least until their building is sold.

The experience of Lakeside Church illustrates why it is best to worship in a neutral location from day one of the merger. Lakeside Church decided they could make one of their existing buildings work for the newly merged church. When they were warned that their choice of location would cause conflict and division, people from the merging churches maintained that they had a commitment to the vision. However, within six weeks, some were grumbling about the choice of facility, stating that one of the other facilities had been more handicap accessible even though the facility had little parking space and was costly to upkeep. Because the facility that was chosen was not accessible and prevented those in wheelchairs from entering the sanctuary, the Lakeside Church moved to an elementary school for worship within four months. It was at that point that the new church began to experience a sense of unity and community.

Questions often arise around "our stuff" and legacy issues. Vital Mergers have addressed these issues in different and creative ways. Stained glass windows from merging churches have been removed from the old buildings to be placed in the new building. A tag sale was held for all the churches of one merger, with the proceeds going toward the building fund. Several of the mergers let family members claim memorial gifts and the remainder of the items were either used in the new building or sold. One of the mergers created a heritage room, which became a common area for fellowship with displays of historical items from each of the churches.

Building issues are often the greatest concern and biggest obstacle a Vital Merger faces. Once this issue is settled, the new building is one of the greatest unifying factors for the new congregation.

Money Matters

Churches that are considering merging are concerned about money matters such as where the money will come from to build a new building, how they will raise the funds, and the cost of the new facilities. These are legitimate concerns and questions. People involved in the merger process may be hesitant to move forward with the merger because of financial considerations.

Many churches considering a Vital Merger are struggling to survive and make decisions based on scarcity mentality. These people cannot envision a time when they would have enough money to do ministry, let alone have enough to buy land or build a new facility. Some have difficulty wrapping their minds around the idea that one new, well-designed, energy-efficient building will cost less to operate than the two, three, or four buildings they already own. Plus, they will save money by eliminating duplicate staffing and programming costs.

Initially, some money for a facility will come from the sale of existing properties. Some will come from endowments and savings that the churches have. The bulk of the money will need to be raised through a capital funds campaign. A company specializing in capital campaigns should be used to raise these funds. Many churches will think they can do it in-house and avoid paying the high prices of the campaign companies. However, the do-it-in-house approach usually fails to raise the needed capital for the new building.

Money Questions

- How will we raise the money to move immediately into a construction phase?
- How will we raise the money to build a new building?
- Who will control our endowments?

Although there are no guarantees, most companies specializing in church capital campaigns maintain that they can increase giving. The Evangelical Lutheran Church of America (ELCA) encourages churches to use their Stewardship Department, claiming that a congregation can raise 250 percent of their annual giving.[21]

Volkart May and Associates, a marketing and research firm in Minneapolis-St. Paul, Minnesota, conducted a study of more than 1,000 churches across the United States who had recently completed capital campaigns. The study shows that churches that did their own campaigns raised, on average, 1.7 times their church's annual gift income compared with those who utilized professional help who raised an average of 2.30 times the contribution income from members.[22]

Another financial concern is deciding who will control the endowment money or savings in the new church. In a Vital Merger—or any merger for that matter—all funds should be included in the merger and become property of the new church. Money should not be withheld. In one traditional merger, one of the churches secretly held back funds and used their money to leverage decisions. Whenever this group wanted to make a building improvement and the Leadership Team or Finance Team disagreed, they would use their hidden stash to complete the project anyway. They also funded programs that did not follow the mission of the new church, creating a conflicting sense of direction for members in the new church. It is not surprising that this merger dissolved within two years.

Arrangement Concerns

Questions about the structure of the new church are on the minds of many people whose churches are considering a merger. A common question is, "How can we prevent our smaller church from being swallowed up by the larger church in the merger?" One of the commitments for a successful Vital Merger is that no church has majority leadership representation post-merger (See Chapter 1). If any of the churches are allowed to have a superior role in the merger process, resistance will arise and cause increased conflict. Establishing a rule that all churches have equal representation on all major decision-making

Arrangement Questions

- How can we prevent the larger church in the merger from swallowing up our church?
- How do we decide which employees to keep, and who gets laid off?

boards or committees during the first two years of the merger helps to eliminate many of the concerns about being swallowed up or taken over.

People also want to know what will happen to the employees who have served their church for years. These employees are often dearly loved, and the congregation values their service. This concern has the potential to create conflict and hard feelings. While it must be honestly communicated that employees will not be guaranteed a position in the newly merged church, it must be made equally clear that all employees will be cared for with grace, and will receive a fair severance package based on years of service.

Time and Patience

How long does the merger process take? Some people may fear that they will be rushed into making a decision without time to think through all the issues, or with little time to get to know people from the other merging churches. Generally, once the merger discussions begin, the process usually takes six to twelve months. Sometimes, mergers take longer. At Living Hope Church, Pastor Linda said the process took three years because most of the time was focused on building relationships and determining if they wanted to follow through with the merger process.

Time Questions

- How soon will the merger happen?
- How long does the merger process take?

The Fellowship Church Vital Merger spent more than two years ensuring that the people understood the Vital Merger process, gaining trust in each other, and growing in their love and acceptance of each other. New Life Church took more than five years to build agreement and make a decision to merge.

The Vital Merger process allows people time to explore and work through concerns about the merger. One of the dangers of moving too quickly is that the churches won't have a dating period—a time of building relationships. Just as with a

Leader Tip

There is no set formula about how many straw polls to conduct. Most of the Vital Mergers have conducted at least one straw poll, while one Vital Merger conducted three. Many reported that this was a positive experience that revealed areas of concern that needed to be addressed. In one church, members voiced their opposition to a merger through a straw poll. The merger team listened to the people and addressed their objections so well that the congregation finally voted to merge with 78 percent in favor.

dating couple considering marriage, if churches haven't built healthy relationships and a comfortable level of familiarity with each other before they tackle the bigger tasks and concerns of the merger, they won't have the knowledge and trust to walk through this new commitment together as a functional, healthy new church. The people of all the churches involved in the merger need to know each other, evaluate their core values and goals, and decide if they can work with each before they enter into the actual merger relationship.

Leadership Challenges

A major concern for leaders is losing people in the merger process. Pastor Joe of New Life Church said that they lost approximately 25 percent of members from the two churches during the merger process. He adds, "However, throughout the whole process we watched new people come in a little faster than others left. We are now even seeing a few who have left returning to the congregation."

Leadership Questions:

- What percentage of people will we lose in the merger process?
- Will our pastor get to stay?
- Who will be the pastor of this new church?

Losing 25 percent of the congregation is a higher loss than most mergers have experienced. Based on observations of several mergers, most Vital Mergers may experience an initial loss of approximately 10-15 percent of their combined membership. Lakeside and The Connection churches lost less than 10 percent, while Living Hope lost about 15 percent, The Vine lost 20 percent, Fellowship and Next Steps lost less than 5 percent of their active members.

Of course, churches do not want to lose members. Churches want to hold on to every member. These people have worshiped and served together. The Vital Merger process offers an opportunity for members to explore their reasons for membership in their local church and for theological reflection regarding the purpose, mission, and vision of their church.

Pastors of Vital Mergers have observed that many of the people who leave do so because they were not able to exercise as much control over the church's focus, programs, and direction. For years they have called the shots. Many have been well-intentioned gatekeepers, but have kept the church from moving into a healthier and more relevant ministry. When these people leave, those who remain often experience the freedom to move in new directions and into new ministries to which they have felt God's calling for some time.

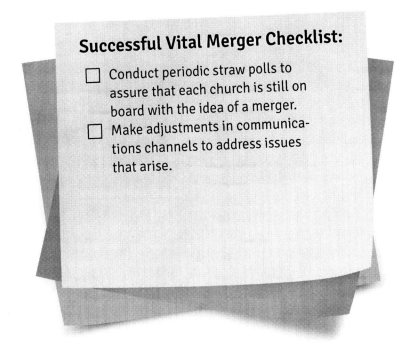

Successful Vital Merger Checklist:

☐ Conduct periodic straw polls to assure that each church is still on board with the idea of a merger.

☐ Make adjustments in communications channels to address issues that arise.

The Prenuptial:
Writing the
Merger Document

Prenuptial agreement (antenuptial agreement) n. a written contract between two people who are about to marry, setting out the terms of possession of assets, treatment of future earnings, and control of the property.[23]

WHEN A COUPLE STARTS THINKING ABOUT MARRIAGE AND ALL the issues and details of joining their lives and blending their families, a lot is at stake. Many romantics are turned off by the notion of a prenuptial because a contract seems cold and pessimistic, opposite of the loving feeling that is leading them toward the altar. However, a good prenuptial allows the couple to understand the boundaries and parameters of the arrangement in a way that wine and roses cannot. Like couples carefully preparing a life together by using a prenuptial, churches merging together outline the details, conditions, and agreements of their merger through a merger document. Effective merger documents outline the basic terms of the merger without creating a lengthy document that is overly binding or cumbersome to read.

While clarifying the terms, the merger document can be an effective tool that helps unify the churches. Pastor Linda from Living Hope Church explained that the merger document helped the congregations blend together because it clearly stated the process of forming committees and choosing committee chairs so that the churches had equal representation. Choosing a new name early in the process helped to build a sense of community as the churches focused on joint social activities, picnics, Bible studies, and fundraising. The merger document helped the congregations work together as a new congregation and gain focus on fulfilling God's plan at Living Hope.

The merger document consists of nine items: purpose, name, mission statement, programs, structure, staffing, property concerns, financial assets and liabilities, and timeline. A section outlining the Resolution and Acceptance should conclude the merger document. Other areas of focus should not be included in the merger document.

Purpose

This section of the document outlines the reasons that the merger is taking place. Although in some cases the financial situations of the churches have led to the merger discussion, it is hoped that as the meetings have continued, the people have moved beyond the financial considerations to a mission focus on what God wants to do through them as a new church. The Purpose section may include a brief two or three-paragraph history of the churches that provides a historical grounding to the document and affirming the heritage of the congregations included in the merger. The Purpose section also notes the similarities of the churches, outlines what the joint ministry will accomplish, explains the advantages of merging, and states future plans for the church as they begin a new life together.

Name

The name of the new church should be clearly stated. It should not be a name taken from any of the churches merging. In other words, if First Church and Grace Church are merging, the new name cannot be First Grace Church or Grace First Church. The new name can and should reflect the new identity they are forming together. It may echo a significant scripture that has guided the church during the merger process, such as River of Life ("Then the angel showed me the river of the water of life, as clear as crystal, flowing from the throne of God and of the Lamb down the middle of the great street of the city." Revelation 22:1-2). Or, it may state an intended outcome or attitude this new ministry will inspire, such as New Hope or New Life.

The Living Hope Church merger document outlines the process used to find a new name for their church.

A Word of Caution

A judicatory official should not decide the name of the new church. The process of choosing a name helps people in the merging congregations build a sense of community, identity, and purpose. Therefore, they should discern this and name their church.

As a result of Visioning Committee meetings, with both churches in attendance, several names for the new church were presented to both congregations for consideration. After several weeks of discernment, a ballot vote was taken at each church. The congregation felt drawn to Colossians 1:3-5 (NLT) in which Paul says, "We always pray for you, and we give thanks to God, the Father of our Lord Jesus Christ. For we have heard of your faith in Christ Jesus and your love for all of God's people, which come from your confident hope of what God has reserved for you in heaven. You have had this expectation ever since you first heard the truth of the Good News." This scripture provided hope that God would be present with them during the merger process, as well as help them reach the people of the surrounding community through their faith, witness, and service.

Mission Statement

The Mission or Purpose Statement should give clarity and direction to the new church. All ministries and programs that the new church begins should flow from or fulfill the mission statement. One of the major reasons that the old, existing programs of the previous churches are not automatically continued in the new church is that they may not follow or support the new vision.

Those writing the merging document should resist cutting and pasting from mission statements of leading churches. For example, Willow Creek Community Church in South Barrington, Illinois, has this mission statement: "To turn irreligious people into fully devoted followers of Jesus Christ." Saddleback Church in Southern California, states their purpose: "To lead people to Jesus and membership in his family, teach them to worship the Lord and magnify his name, develop them to Christlike maturity, and equip them for ministry in the church, and a mission in the world." Ginghamsburg church in Tipp City, Ohio, outlines their statement in a simpler way:

Bring – seeking people into a life-CELEBRATION with Jesus
Grow – as disciples in CELL community
Serve – out of our CALL and giftedness

Because these statements have been effective in guiding these successful churches, a new church may be tempted to simply adopt one of these statements, or one similar, without doing the work of seeking God for the specific direction for their new ministry. The mission statement must carefully reflect the discerned direction in which God is leading the Vital Merger to new ministry as a new church.

Programs

The programs should flow out of the church's mission. Longtime members of the merging churches may suggest retaining all, or at least many, of the programs that were offered by the churches prior to the merger.

Some of the programs probably began many years earlier as a result of a specific need in the church or community. As times change, community needs also change. Old programs may have lost their urgency and effectiveness, and they may not contribute to the mission of the new church.

One church located in an urban setting hosted a soup kitchen pre-merger to serve the community's need. When this church merged with other churches, they moved to a different neighborhood with different demographics. The merging churches agreed that the soup kitchen was important and some members were committed to the ministry. However, to fully honor their new mission statement, the newly merged church decided that the soup kitchen was not where the church needed to focus its energy and resources.

Despite the decision that was made, the newly merged church yielded to pressure from members who had participated in the soup kitchen ministry and kept the soup kitchen open. However, keeping the soup kitchen involved continuing to own the church building in which this ministry operated, including upkeep, utilities, and other expenses that drained resources from other ministries.

Think About It

A pastor of one Vital Merger explains that the merger document helped to blend both congregations by stating the make up of the committees with equal numbers from both churches being assigned. The choosing of a new name early in the process gave focus and participation in social activities, picnics, Bible studies, fund-raising activities, and joint participation in the planning of a new building. This helped to blend the two congregations.

Finally, as the church continued to pray about supporting the soup kitchen, another church moved into the vicinity of the soup kitchen. This ministry also had a mission and vision for a soup kitchen. The Vital Merger was able to share supplies, start-up equipment, and some financial assistance. The collaboration also allowed the members of the Vital Merger who had a commitment to the soup kitchen ministry to continue to serve there. The Vital Merger was then able to sell the church building and use the capital for their new facility.

Structure

Human nature tends to hold on to what is familiar and comfortable. When it comes to structure, church members may want to retain the structure that has been in existence for years. In many cases, the structure is bloated and dysfunctional. The structure was likely implemented years earlier, in most cases when the size of the church was larger. Over time, additional at-large positions were added, increasing the size of the ruling board.

Where the polity of a denomination specifies the constituency of the leadership board, the lag time of denominational change may result in a recommended model that is outdated and ineffective. A more functional structure for ministry today is a smaller and more nimble leadership team. The team should represent the major ministry areas of the church. A smaller leadership team facilitates the launching and overseeing of new ministries more effectively, and promotes a permission-giving rather than permission-withholding climate for ministry.

Staffing

The Vital Merger Team will need to decide how to staff the new church. Altogether, many people may have been employed by the merging churches including secretaries, choir directors, accompanists, and custodians, as well as other ministry leaders who cannot all be employed in the new church. The merger document must clearly outline what staff positions the new ministry requires and how many people the new church will employ.

The merger document does not need to outline hiring practices, but the Merger Team should discuss the hiring process. The new personnel committee (or its equivalent, depending upon the polity of the denomination) should meet soon after the merger is approved to determine the process for hiring new employees.

The Vital Merger Team must consider its anticipated new size and determine how many clergy are needed and how they will function together. Many of the Vital Mergers involve small churches, each with only one pastor. Merger Team members may be familiar only with small-church structures and will think in terms of one pastor. However, the new merged church may be a mid-sized or large church that requires more than one pastor.

This was clearly the case with several Vital Mergers, and Fellowship Church is a good example. The three churches that merged had an average worship attendance of sixty, eighty-seven, and ninety-one, with a combined attendance of 230. The three churches were staffed with two full-time pastors and one three-quarter time pastor. The Merger Team had determined that they only needed one full-time pastor to meet all the ministry and leadership needs of the new church. Pastoral care consumed much of the pastor's time, and he had little time to focus on vision casting, creating a new congregational culture, and reaching out to the unchurched people of the community. The pastor was able to bring on additional staff several months after the merger, and within two years the worship attendance grew to 272. The Merger Team must consider the size and increased demands of the new church to determine its leadership needs.

Property Concerns

The Vital Merger document states that all churches are to sell all property (with the exception of needed parsonages), move into a neutral location for worship, and begin the process of purchasing new property and/or building. The merger document outlines the process in which this will occur and specifies the timeline that will be used. In other words, it will clearly define how the buildings will be sold and which parsonages will be retained. It may specify that a commercial realtor will be used to sell the buildings.

In most cases the merger document will not include the property to be purchased or the kind of building to be built. This is for the new, merged church to determine. The merger document will include the

Leader Tip

Town hall style meetings held throughout the document writing process provide a venue for addressing issues and concerns. The laity of the Merger Team give the general overview of the Vital Merger, steps involved, and progress completed to date. A question and answer session follows the presentation allowing people to make speeches as well as submit their questions to be read aloud and answered by the Merger Team. A free and open debate allows all voices to be heard. At the conclusion of the town hall meeting a straw poll can be taken.

make-up of the new Site-location Team or Building Team, but not bind their work by providing too much direction.

There are exceptions. In the Next Steps Church merger, the church was purchasing a church building as part of the merger. The purchase was agreed upon before the merger, and was a part of the overall plan. The new building was located about ten miles from the previous congregations, which put the new church in a new community and, therefore, in a new mission field.

Financial Assets and Liabilities

The merger document outlines the manner in which finances will be conducted. In this document, all the financial obligations and assets must be disclosed. All parties in the merger must know what they are inheriting—for better or for worse. All accounts need to be audited before the merger takes place. Any specially designated funds need to be clearly outlined and the merger document should provide a clear understanding of how these accounts will be used in the merged church.

In one merger (not a Vital Merger, but an arranged marriage by a judicatory official), there was a lack of trust between the two churches, as well as a lack of unified vision. Therefore, both congregations retained their endowment monies. When one of the congregations proposed a project and the joint leadership team voted against it, the congregation that was in favor of the project funded it themselves.

In another merger, the proposal to purchase a projector was initiated from a committee composed mostly of members from one church. The Leadership Team voted against it. In response, the committee funded the projector from undisclosed endowment money, had it installed mid-week, and the new projector was ready for use when the congregation came to worship on Sunday morning. Needless to say, secrets and power plays cause deep mistrust and resentment in a church. There can be no unified vision when factions of the church are using money as a weapon against other factions in the church.

The merger documents will outline how the finances of the church will be administered once the merger has taken place. Part of the work of the Administrative Team is to provide a budget for the new church. The budget is not to be included in the merger document. However, it must be completed prior to the merger so that the new church has a sound financial plan.

Timeline

The timeline used for the Vital Merger should be outlined in the merger document. The timeline states the date of the Celebration Sunday (the uniting celebration of the merging churches). An ideal situation would be if the pastors of the merging churches leave by the week prior to the Celebration Sunday, and a new pastor begins on Celebration Sunday. In some cases this new pastor will be an interim pastor as the Pulpit Committee calls the new church-planting pastor.

Once the merger document is complete, a local attorney, who understands local and state laws and who has experience with merging corporations, should be retained to review the merger document.

Sample Documents

A sample merger document for churches to use as a guideline is found in Appendix 2. Churches should not cut-and-paste from the sample document, or simply change the wording to be appropriate for its own context. The Merger Team must do the hard work of communicating and gaining an understanding between all parties involved for the merger document to be relevant and aid in the success of the merger itself.

Successful Vital Merger Checklist

☐ Develop a merger document that outlines the details of the new church (see sample merger document in Appendix 2)

☐ Send a copy of each draft of the merger document to the appropriate judicatory official and staff person responsible for church planting.

☐ Hold town hall style meetings to inform all congregations of the progress of the merger document and to answer questions concerning the future of the church.

☐ Have an attorney review the merger document for legal purposes.

☐ Forward the completed merger document to appropriate judicatory officials.

☐ Make the completed copy of the merger document available to members of each church for study and discussion.

☐ Contact a judicatory official (if applicable) to authorize a church conference or congregational meeting for the Merger Vote.

CHAPTER
8

Popping the Question: Will You Merge With Me— Yes or No?

AFTER MUCH DATING, COMMUNICATING, TESTING THE WATERS, and detailing the prenuptial agreement, it is time for the proposal. Although answering "yes" to a proposal of marriage usually precedes the writing of the prenuptial, the actual decision to follow through with the marriage is made after the prenuptial is completed. When churches are considering a Vital Merger, there comes a time when the merger document has been completed, the congregations' questions have been answered, and the people must decide if they want to move into the future as one united congregation. In the Vital Merger process, the next step is the vote when church members say "yes" or "no" to the Vital Merger. The voting should take place at a church conference or an all-church meeting.

The voting procedure should be discussed, agreed upon, and clearly outlined before the vote is taken. All churches should vote on the same day. Sometimes it is possible for everyone to vote at the same time, but more often churches vote one after the other, in succession, throughout the same day. The votes are always taken at a congregational meeting (for United Methodists this is a Church Conference). This meeting is usually led by a judicatory official, such as a District Superintendent. No votes are counted until all the churches have voted. At that time, the official will count the votes, with the counting witnessed by members of the Merger Team. A two-thirds majority vote in each individual church, rather than a simple majority, is recommended for the merger to be approved. A sample Vital Merger Ballot is found in Appendix 3. It is generally best to provide the same ballot for all of the churches. Sometimes, one or more of the churches vote against the merger. Perhaps, the church does not want to lose its identity, its control over its own future, or its financial endowments. Hard feelings between some members of the churches, sentimentality about the building or history, fear of change, and lack of trust may also lead to a "no" vote. A pastor from one of the mergers stated:

> *Several people opposed to the Vital Merger contacted a select group of people about two to three weeks prior to the final vote, twisted the truth about the Vital Merger, and created a scenario far from the truth. They claimed the clergy had been sent by "The Conference" to shut them all down – that we had skewed the numbers to make it all seem far more dire than it actually was, and that we only wanted to make a big mega church so we'd get all the glory, etc.*

No one was surprised that this church voted "no" on the Vital Merger.

In one merger, a church participated in the process until the vote, but did not vote to merge. Several of the members had developed hard feelings toward people in one of the other churches during their years of sharing the same pastor, and others were simply attached to the building and wanted their funerals to be held at that church. In another merger, the church wanted to stay in control of the large endowment they received before the merger process began.

Fear of change is most often the underlying motive for not moving ahead. However, for some, opposition originates from truly altruistic motives such as the recognition that a merger would eliminate a church that has had a significant impact in reaching a segment of the community that the larger, merged church will probably not reach. For example, an African-American church voted not to be involved because of their noteworthy history. They were afraid that they would lose an important reminder of their ethnic heritage if they were to sell their building in a merger.

For a few of the Vital Mergers, one or more of the churches involved in the merger discussions failed to get the two-thirds majority vote required to pass the merger. In the Connection merger, the Fourth Street Church thought they could derail the entire merger by voting against it. They voted it down while the other two churches approved the merger. The next day the other two churches met and asked the question, "Would their two churches move forward with a merger, or would they scrap the idea?" They decided that since their churches had voted in favor of the Vital Merger, they would proceed. Once the people at Fourth Street Church realized that the merger was moving ahead without them, they reconsidered and set a date for another merger vote, which they approved by 80 percent.

Think About It

What do you wish had been done differently?

I wish we had taken one more year to build support so all four churches were on board with the merger. Pressure to "get it done" by Judicatory leaders created "push" in the minds of the membership that this merger was driven by the conference.

**Pastor Ethan,
Calvary Church**

Having a provision in the merger document stating how many of the churches would need to approve the merger for the process to move forward would have helped Fourth Street Church to contribute earlier and be more proactive in the merger process. Generally, as long as two or more of the churches vote in favor of the merger, the merger should proceed with the churches that approve the merger.

The Lakeside Church merger originally included four churches in the merger discussion. The merger vote resulted in three out of the four churches voting to merge. One of the churches, St. Paul's, passed the vote by a margin of 55 percent, failing to receive the two-thirds required for passage. At a later time, St. Paul's reconsidered joining the merger, but again failed to receive the votes to merge.

Think About It

What do you wish had been done differently?

I wish we had not had so many casualties. However, I do not believe we would have come this far if very many of those persons had stayed in our church. Most of the people who left went to one of two small congregations in our community.

**Pastor Joe,
New Life Church**

When churches begin to consider a Vital Merger, they should also clean their membership records. Inclusion of inactive members in the voting process can be problematic.[24] For example, during the New Life Church Vital Merger, the first time the two churches voted on the merger it was approved by Central Church by 70 percent, but Bethany Church missed the two-thirds majority by only one vote. Bethany members expressed frustration that twenty-one inactive members showed up to vote no. At that time, the regional conference of their denomination required that the church wait for one year before they could hold another vote for a merger. They continued discussing the merger throughout the year that followed, and both churches approved the second vote—Bethany by 70 percent and Central by 75 percent.

This same scenario occurred at the Fellowship merger. A group of inactive members showed up at Zion Church for the vote that was being held before worship. The active members were shocked and disappointed at the attitudes and actions of the dissenting group. As soon as the vote was cast, most of the inactive members, some who had not been in attendance for more than twenty years, got up and left the sanctuary. They did not care to participate in the church with their prayers, presence, gifts, service, or witness. They did not care to worship, yet they wanted to control the future of the church. The vote to merge passed by a simple majority (by one vote), but failed to meet the two-thirds needed for acceptance.

The fall-out at Zion Church was significant. The majority of the congregation felt betrayed because a few disgruntled members brought inactive members to vote rather than work through their concerns in open discussion. Most of the congregation believed the merger process was in the best interest of the church as well as the leading of God. They, unlike the inactive members, had participated in prayerful discernment and believed God's leading and blessing had been integral to the entire process. As a result, about one-half of the congregation of Zion Church left that church to be part of the new Fellowship Church, even before its official opening on July 1.

In another merger, a pastor whose church voted "no" described the fall-out that occurred when people with differences of opinion and core values struggled with each other concerning the direction of the church's ministry:

> My church lost a good chunk of its congregation. Folks who voted 'yes' were in turmoil for a few weeks. Some folks walked and never looked back and started attending one of the other churches. Some folks tried to stay for a while, but couldn't deal with the comments and attitudes of those who voted 'no.' Some folks stuck it out until July because they didn't want to abandon me with the folks who voted 'no,' and who were not happy I was staying around until July. Ultimately most, if not all, of the folks who voted 'yes,' left between November and July. There was a lot of mudslinging – about me and about the 'yes'-voters and anyone else who was in favor of the Vital Merger. Comments were made about 'yes' voters, calling them 'Traitors' and 'Worthless, Evil, Church Killers'.

In this particular church, the Merger Team and the majority of the congregation supported the Vital Merger. Unfortunately those opposed to the merger urged inactive members to vote "no". Thus, the final vote was skewed and did not reflect the will of the majority engaged in active ministry.

Sometimes, after the church has voted against the merger and people begin to realize that they have lost a significant number of their congregation to the merged church, the leadership of the dissenting church decides that they need to merge after all. Several months after Fellowship Church began, some of the leaders of the Zion church approached the leaders of Fellowship Church about joining the merger. However, after more discussion, it became clear that the remaining members of Zion Church had a different vision and attitude about ministry than that of Fellowship Church. The dissenting church made many demands regarding the structure and wanted to alter the vision and direction of Fellowship Church. Therefore, Fellowship Church decided that a merger with Zion would not work.

The Vital Merger process may reveal opposing core values that may cause people to decide that they can no longer engage in ministry together. Although such decisions are difficult, they can be a catalyst for strengthened faith and positive change through prayer. It is hard for people to accept that members are leaving their church, but those who leave a failing church to engage in a new work often find a setting where their passion and skills can bear fruit and are not stretched so thin that they risk burnout.

Think About It

What do you wish had been done differently?

We should have done it differently by getting the same information to each congregation, making sure we, as clergy, were on the same page, stopping wild rumors and getting the same advice from all the judicatory leaders.

**Pastor Betsy,
Water of Life Church**

Churches who are considering a merger should review their membership records and remove those who are "negligent of the vows or regularly absent from the worship of the church without valid reason"[25] prior to moving into the merger discussions.[26] By removing inactive members (or at least starting this process) at the beginning of the merger discussions, the church can be assured that more or most of those voting on the Vital Merger will be part of the prayerful discernment and thoughtful discussion prior to the vote.

Churches with a congregational style of governance may not have a clearly defined method of removing members. Churches in the Vital Merger process should research their procedures for removing inactive (or non-participatory) members from their roles. In the Vital Merger document, they should specify who may vote with guidelines for this issue in their future congregational by-laws.

Regarding dissenting churches reconsidering the Vital Merger, the dissenting church can ask to be adopted by the Vital Merger. In an adoption, members of the church putting itself up for adoption must understand that they will need to follow the rules and integrate the values of the adopting church. There are no negotiations around the mission, vision, and direction upon which the new church has agreed. The adopted church must accept the fact that they missed forming the direction of this new church. Further, the adopted church cannot expect an equal number of their leadership to be represented on each board, committee, or team. They forfeited all these rights when they originally voted no.

After engaging in honest and open conversation, most churches are in favor of mergers. Prayer and Christian conversation can invite God's healing and instill unity of Spirit as people follow God's call for their church. During the engagement period to come, those who had reservations will begin to see the possibilities of this new church. They will begin to understand the new DNA and vision of the new church and start building deeper relationships with the people in their new church community.

After months or maybe years of praying, dreaming, planning, discussing, dating, and many meetings, churches decide to vote on the merger. In most cases, this is a wonderful time of celebration as the churches now begin to look ahead to a new life together as a new church. However, there is much work to be done during the transition process.

Leader Tip

How to deal with a church that votes "No".

Sometimes one of the churches votes "no" to the Vital Merger. How do the churches who voted "yes" respond to the church that voted "no"? The simple answer is with grace and respect.

When one of the churches votes "no" to the merger, much pain exists for everyone. The churches that voted in favor of the merger are excited about their own future, and at first cannot imagine their life as a new church without the people from the other church. Because people from each of the congregations have built strong relationships with people in the other churches, some may feel rejected, as though they were "left at the altar."

In addition, the people from the church that voted "no" are often split. Many in the church had hopes of moving on in their life as part of the new Vital Merger. They may have served on the Merger Team, attended merger meetings and town-hall events, and voted in the straw poll. In many ways, they were already transferring their allegiance to the new church. Others, however, felt equally as strong that they wanted to continue as an individual church, continuing to do ministry in their community as they have for many years. They also attended meetings, prayed, and wanted the best for their congregation.

Often when one of the churches votes "no," many from that church leave anyway to move on to the new church. When Zion Church voted on the merger, the congregation was split almost evenly. The final vote was 51 percent for the merger, 49 percent against it. For Eureka Road Church, the outcome was much different. They voted in favor of the merger by 63 percent, but failed to reach the required 66 percent for approval. In both instances, almost half of the church members left to become a part of the Vital Merger. In both cases, the people coming to the Vital Merger were welcomed and the leaders from those congregations were placed in leadership positions. Those remaining in the non-merging churches do well to use this time of transition to examine their existing mission and vision and to discern the best use of their resources for effective ministry.

Successful Vital Merger Checklist

☐ Define and communicate who is eligible to vote before the vote is taken. Each tribe may have different rules. For example, in a United Methodist Church/Charge Conference the following people have a vote:
  - Professing members (those who have taken membership as professions of faith or by transfer)

  - Retired ministers and diaconal ministers who hold their charge conference membership at the church
  - Affiliate members[27]

☐ Take the vote. Set the bar for approval at two-thirds (66 percent) of those voting to insure that a larger percentage of the congregation is in support of the merger.[28]

CHAPTER
9

Engagement: Congregational Transition Time

THE COUPLE HAS DATED AND THE WARM, FUZZY FEELINGS STILL linger. They have considered what the future looks like for them (thinking about marriage, getting a prenuptial), the families have gotten to know one another, the proposal was accepted, and the engagement ring given. In the midst of the excitement about their new life together, they have some major planning to do. Not only do they need to start planning their wedding ceremony, but they need to examine their financial resources, decide where they will rent or buy a home that fits their present needs, continue discussing how their core values and future dreams will be lived out, and begin living into the reality of life together. All of this with the knowledge that as they work toward their wedding day, they will say goodbye to the single life and embrace a new married life together.

Likewise, when churches finally say "I do" to the Vital Merger, they enter a time of preparing for the realities and transition together. The transition, or engagement period, is a time to create the new congregational culture, to begin forming the new DNA, and to begin acting as a united congregation with a new identity. It is an exciting time of looking forward to the celebration and the lifetime together that follows. Generally, this transition time lasts from three to six months.

During this transition time, the Merger Team begins implementing the merger document, which includes forming new committees or teams; finalizing what staff will be hired, retained, or discontinued; preparing a new church budget; determining the neutral location for worship; and assigning or calling the new pastor. In addition, congregations will probably worship several times together, choirs or bands may begin rehearsing together, and the church will begin to move more and more in the direction of becoming one congregation. However, the churches will not "move in together" at this time. They will wait for a celebration of the merger before they unify as one congregation.

As a part of their engagement, one Vital Merger was excited to share their newly forming church with the community. Although the merger was several months away, the people were planning their first Christmas Eve Candlelight service together. They planned to worship in a school auditorium for the Christmas Eve service and hoped the new location would attract first-time guests. Attendance at the individual churches was between 50 to 75 at each Candlelight service. For the Christmas Eve combined service they had more than 450 in attendance, including many first-time attendees. The choir had more than 50 singers. The combined worship service affirmed their decision and efforts to merge.

During the engagement time, many in the church dream about the ministries that will soon be possible as they live and work together as a new church. While dreaming together, the churches forming Fellowship Church realized that many people in their community did not have hot meals. Some in the merging churches wanted to provide a ministry of hot meals, but the individual churches never had the resources—people or financial—to begin this new ministry. Fellowship Church, while still in the engagement phase, began a new ministry to meet the needs of their community, including a free hot meal served Friday evenings.

Though engagement is an exciting time of possibility, it can also be a time of trials. During the course of their engagement, a couple will begin to discover some differences in values and lifestyle as well as in personality and preferences. One may be a planner while the other may be more spontaneous. One may value couple-time more than the other does. One may be a collector while the other is a cleaner. One may desire a large family with a home in the country while the other may prefer to delay having children and enjoy the energy of city life. Differences may arise around issues such as work, time management, budgeting, food, and decorating. One may prefer a short engagement and a simple wedding so they can start their life together sooner. The other may need more time planning and prefer a large, more traditional church wedding. The way the couple handles conflicts (e.g., creatively and lovingly, or selfishly and destructively), will shape their relationship.

During the transition period, the Merger Team must prayerfully discern and carefully articulate how the churches are planning to live together as one. How difficulties are handled is crucial to the health of the new church. When issues arise, will the congregations find creative ways of addressing them, or will they fall into old patterns of unhealthy communication? Focusing together on gratitude for all God has done and cultivating openness to what God will do in their midst will unify the congregations and help them resist temptations to take shortcuts, form factions, and hold on to ineffective structures and practices.

Careful transitioning is essential to the health of a Vital Merger. Excellent resources are available about the theories and practices of healthy transitions.[29] The following are examples offering practical advice for navigating through some transitional issues.

Leadership Structure

Defining the leadership structure and the nomination or election of the new leaders is crucial to having buy-in from all the merged churches. All new leaders must be in agreement with the Vital Merger as well as view the newly merged church as a new church start. They cannot rely on past traditions or familiar ways of leading the church. The merger must be viewed by the leaders as a new day for ministry.

The new nominating team must make sure the newly formed teams have equal representation from each church. Parity is more important than proportion. Some pastors and church leaders have argued that the leadership should be proportional (the larger church having a larger proportion of leaders, etc.) However, proportional representation may lead to one church exerting more control. An important commitment to a successful Vital Merger is making every effort to have equal representation for the first two years (See Chapter 1). By the end of the second year, if the merger has proceeded in an equitable manner, the new church should be experiencing an overall sense of unity and cohesiveness where people identify less with their previous churches and more as members of a new, unified church.

The new leadership structure should be small, simple, and nimble. The merger is a great time to discard the old, 1950's structure dependent upon many chairs of committees attending monthly meetings to give a report or seek permission to do ministry. Instead, the new church should begin with a simple leadership style made up of a few permission-giving leaders whose primary purpose is keeping the church focused on their vision. Likewise, teams should be focused on mission and ministry instead of attending administrative meetings and giving reports.[30]

Staffing Needs

When the Merger Team considers staffing the new church, it should do so with a focus on growth. Many of the churches seeking a Vital Merger are smaller congregations staffed with one pastor, maybe a part-time choir director, pianist, or youth leader. The Merger Team must recognize that a lingering mindset may be to focus on retaining one pastor with limited staffing. After the merger, the new church must acknowledge its transition from a small, single-cell church to a larger church with significant potential and ability to broaden ministry. The newly merged church needs to recognize that the church has more people and will require multiple staff positions to accommodate the change. For example, the merged church may need a full-time pastor, an associate pastor, or several part-time staff specialists. The church should consider a full-time worship leader or worship arts leader as they start new worship services. A pastor of Congregational Care would also free the lead pastor for vision casting and focusing on the health and growth of the new church.

Trinity Church merged with three churches, each averaging 140, 140, and 350 to one congregation with an average worship attendance of 600. During their engagement period they restructured staffing to better meet their mission and vision. Instead of simply adding an Associate Pastor to the staff, they hired a specialist in Marriage and Family Counseling, and another associate specializing in Missions and Outreach. They also hired a Communications and Marketing specialist.

Think About It

Churches handle the many artifacts and memorial gifts in a variety of ways. Trinity Church collected some of the meaningful artifacts from each of the churches and displayed them in a Memory Hall located at the primary entrance to the building.

One of the painful decisions during the engagement period is deciding which staff members to keep and which to let go. Some employees have been serving their church for many years, yet they are not well known by the other churches in the merger. They are loved by the members of their church, and in many cases these employees are also members. The new church must make tough decisions and choose people who will offer the best leadership and ministry as they move forward. Before five churches merged into The Journey Church, each church had a part-time music director. As a merged church with average worship attendance of 250, the Journey Church now had resources to hire one gifted and well-trained full-time worship leader.

Each Vital Merger will need to decide how they want to handle staffing issues. Some may decide all employees will apply for the positions in the new church. Some may choose by seniority. Some may receive applications only from former employees, while others will open the interview process to the community. However this is handled, it is important that the process be carefully planned and clearly articulated with grace. Grace also leads to affirmation and generosity; therefore, healthy severance packages should be extended to those who have faithfully served.

Budget

Once married, some couples choose to maintain separate checking and savings accounts. With Vital Mergers all accounts must be consolidated into one single account operated by the new church. During the transition/engagement period, each church continues to manage its own finances while the Finance Team of the new church begins forming the new budget. The Finance Team should consist of the Treasurers and Financial Secretaries of the former churches, as well as other business people. It is imperative that there is complete disclosure of all debts and financial assets.

The Finance Team will discuss and develop a projection of expenses for their first year as a new church. They will consult with the Personnel Team[31] concerning staff compensation; be in conversation with the Location Team concerning expenses related to relocation, office space, and the neutral worship space; and make initial projections of mission and ministry expenses for the new church as well as increased expenses for marketing.

Legal Matters

Certain legal matters must be addressed during the transition period to keep things moving in a timely manner. One matter that must be addressed early in the transition period is listing the buildings for sale. A commercial real estate agent or a real estate agent specializing in the sale of church buildings should be used.

Another matter is changing the deeds of all the properties to reflect the new church name. One Vital Merger, upon the sale of one of their properties, could not close on the sale because the deed had not been

Leader Tip

Adequate staffing is the key to a healthy, successful Vital Merger. For example, hiring a Pastor of Visitation is an important staff position for a Vital Merger. The Pastor of Visitation will focus on pastoral care (visiting the home-bound, making hospital calls, and perhaps organizing and overseeing a care team of lay people). A Pastor of Visitation or Minister of Pastor Care would free the Lead Pastor to focus primarily on developing a new church and reaching new people. The Personnel Team may decide a Worship Director, Music Leader, or Worship Arts Director is needed to coordinate the music and multi-media for worship. Additional secretarial staffing may be needed as well as other staff in the areas of Discipleship, Christian Education, Worship, and Youth. The Personnel Team must envision the needs of the new church when considering staffing for leadership, and they must carefully judge how staffing additions will fulfill the mission of the new church.

changed. The church needed to take the time to file a new deed before they could proceed with the sale.

Incorporation is another matter that needs to be addressed during the transition period. Although the church can use a form downloaded from the internet or purchased at an office supply store, it is best if the church hires an attorney to write this legal document.

Most churches have non-profit postal permits, and these should be changed during the transition period to reflect the new church name. The new church will want to begin marketing their church prior to the Celebration Sunday and prior to moving to their neutral location. A new postal permit will be needed if the church will use direct mail to advertise.

Another important matter is changing the name on the bank accounts, or opening up new accounts reflecting the new name of the church. New checks must be printed. Attention must be given to other financial matters that reflect the names of the churches involved in the merger.[32]

Location

One of the commitments (see Chapter 1) of the Vital Merger is that worship will be conducted at a neutral site beginning with Celebration Sunday. During the transition time as people begin to come to terms with leaving their church building, they may experience tender feelings and possibly some bickering concerning this part of the transition. In a few mergers people have tried to strong-arm the merged church into worshipping in one of the existing sanctuaries.

In one Vital Merger, a group of thirty-four people set up a meeting to make their point with the new pastor. They told the new pastor that they had been told by their former pastor that it was not necessary to move to a neutral location. They finally demanded that the church begin meeting in the church sanctuary (of course in their own sanctuary and not one of the others) or they would all leave the church. The pastor stood his ground, thanked the people for sharing their concern, reiterated why it was necessary to move to a neutral location for the merger to work, and encouraged the people to continue to worship at the neutral location. Some of the people never returned to the church, while others continued to come, but the neutral location was never a major issue after that meeting.

Another Vital Merger's Location Team decided that the new church would not move to a neutral location initially. They were reminded that choosing to worship in a neutral location from the beginning was crucial for the new church's health and growth. However, many of the people loved and cared for each other and were committed to the Vital Merger process (including building a new building in the near future and relocating), and insisted that there would be no conflicts.

Believing they could overcome any issues that might arise regarding some people having to leave their church building while others could stay in their building, they chose to begin worshipping in one of the existing buildings on Celebration Sunday. After one month of worshipping in that building, some people were grumbling and asking why they couldn't alternate between buildings, or why they couldn't move to one of the other buildings. People began to bicker with one another.

To restore relationships, the new church moved to a neutral location and quickly unified around the new mission, focused on reaching new people, conducted a capital campaign, and were able to move into their own, new building debt free.

In a Vital Merger, churches must find a neutral location to worship from Celebration Sunday and onward. A Location Team, established immediately after the merger vote, determines the needs of the church as they search for an interim facility and explore potential sites. Once the best location is identified, the Merger Team is informed and acts on the recommendation.

Some churches may consider leasing space from a larger, existing church nearby. However, renting space from another church can be problematic. The sanctuary reflects values and needs of the host church that may not support the mission and growth of the newly merged church. In addition, the new congregation can become comfortable in its temporary location and lose motivation to have their church home. The Vine Church Vital Merger began worshipping in a facility owned by another denomination. Within a few months, the host congregation invited The Vine to merge with them. Doing so would have complicated the Vital Merger they had worked so hard to support and would have turned it into a traditional merger with the host church, nullifying the benefits of the Vital Merger process.

In addition, the leased church sanctuary may not be conducive to the style of worship that would appeal to the mission field the newly merged church has discerned they are to reach. Worship times may not be optimal because the host church will probably want to conduct their worship service at the most desired time.

Utilizing a different kind of space allows the congregation to experience a different way of worshipping together and maintains the urgency to move forward into their new church home. Schools, community centers, and theaters are good temporary locations. Some churches have leased a store-front facility or a hotel conference room. One leased a closed big-box store and used it for their temporary space.

When looking for a neutral location for worship, the Location Team should find a place that is bright and welcoming. It should be handicap accessible. The facility should provide adequate space for worship and small groups or Sunday school classes to meet. Space for a welcoming center near the entrance and a nursery room close to the worship space are essential. The space should be free from distractions. For example, one church met in a hotel Garden Room with glass walls, located next to the pool. The congregation could not see the videos on the projection screen because of the light coming through the glass walls. The noise and activity of the adjacent pool were also a constant distraction.

The engagement period is a time of decisions that will impact the life of the new church. Leadership structure, staffing needs, budget and financial issues, legal matters, and location are a few of the things that need careful attention during the engagement time.

Successful Vital Merger Checklist

☐ Take care of legal/logistical matters. Begin the process of incorporating, gaining new postal permits, selling buildings, and purchasing a new facility or site for construction of a new building.

10

Engagement: The Role of Pastoral Leadership

DECISIONS SHOULD BE MADE EARLY IN THE ENGAGEMENT PERIOD concerning pastoral leadership. How will the current pastors function during the engagement period? Will a new pastor be called or appointed, or will one of the existing pastors remain? If a new pastor is brought in, when will this happen? How will the new pastor help shape the values and vision of the new church?

The transition time between the vote and the actual merger is a tricky time for clergy leadership. Vital Mergers have smoother transitions and most success when pastors of the merging churches work well with each other and, at the time of the merger, hand the baton to a new, assessed and trained church planting pastor who will lead the newly merged congregation as a new church.

In the United Methodist Church, as well as in some other denominations, the pastor is appointed to lead the new church. In other denominations the pastor is called. Ideally, in the United Methodist Church, the merger should be effective on the official date clergy assignments begin. Churches that "call" their pastor can set an appropriate merger date when the new pastor will arrive.

Some churches or denominations make effective use of intentional interim pastors. Those pastors are assigned or called to the church for a designated period of time, usually not to exceed two years. Use of an intentional interim as a Vital Merger pastor can be very effective if the pastor has a church planting skill-set and training.

Congregations often ask when they can bring the new pastor on board and to what extent the pastor can have input in their new church. This, indeed, can be a difficult dance in which all leadership involved must move forward together. For example, in the United Methodist Church when the pastor is appointed, he or she usually begins the appointment on July 1. The appointment ideally starts on Celebration Sunday in Vital Mergers. Depending on the denomination's protocol, contact from an incoming pastor with the new congregation may be discouraged. However, judicatory authorities must consider the benefits of inviting the new pastor to attend the Merger Team meetings four to six months before the appointment actually begins. As the incoming pastor works closely with the churches and the outgoing pastors during this interim period, he or she gains timely information about the new congregation. The congregation's anxiety is alleviated as they become more comfortable with the new pastor who will be leading their merger.

Pastor Ethan, one of the pastors in the Fellowship Vital Merger, stated how the transition worked in their situation:

We asked that the new pastor be assigned early and work with the ongoing process ASAP to build trust and have input in the developing vision/mission of the new church. It seemed to work well. Perhaps even more time with the incoming pastor could have helped.

Pastor Tom, the new pastor, attended semi-monthly meetings starting in February until July 1, the date his official appointment at Fellowship Church began.

Officials and merging churches must carefully decide whether introducing the new pastor into the process before the Celebration Sunday would be helpful for their particular merger. Allowing the new pastor to attend Merger Team meetings does not work best for all churches, especially when not all of the outgoing pastors are in total agreement with the merger concept or not all are pleased with the choice of the new pastor who will soon arrive.

The Problem with Short Engagement

With some Vital Mergers, the people have been so excited about becoming one church and moving forward in ministry that they want to merge as quickly as possible. It's like the couple who chooses to rush their engagement and move in together without enough time and preparation for the transition.

Problems may occur when congregations merge too soon. An early merger creates a lame-duck time for the pastors who know they will soon be handing leadership to a new pastor. Therefore, some of these pastors may choose not to provide strong leadership in preparing for the merger. Some may feel frustration or grief as they have invested much of their time, patience, gifts, and energy in the merger process, only to be leaving without harvesting the fruit of the merger. Other pastors do not view this transition as a lame duck time, but experience satisfaction in helping their church move into fruitful ministry, and appreciate the experience and skills they acquired in the Vital Merger process.

Churches that merge before a new assessed and trained church-planting pastor is in place to lead them must clearly outline the roles of their current pastors. Lakeside Church Vital Merger had a very short engagement period. They voted in January and merged in February, and they were not prepared for life together with their three current pastors who did not have clearly defined leadership roles. Therefore, there was no clear understanding of who was in charge, which pastor was to do what work, etc. Two of the pastors were strong leaders and were self-appointed to be the lead pastor while the other saw what was coming and simply tried to lay low and miss the shots being fired. To add further tension, one of the pastors began a new worship service without discussing it with the other pastors or the Leadership Team. Confusion ruled. Although worship attendance for the Celebration Sunday was 204, the attendance started declining within two months and dropped to about 160 by the time the new pastor arrived four months later.

Henry, the chairperson of the Vital Merger Team at Lakeside, advised, "We wish we would have formally merged with a new pastor leading us instead of going months with the three current pastors. It was very difficult for the pastors and the congregations. For all kinds of reasons the pastors couldn't /wouldn't lead, the congregations resisted coming together, and, as a result, the merger process stalled." The confusion with clergy leadership roles could have been avoided if the churches had resisted the temptation to shorten their engagement period and had allowed more time for their transition. [33]

Churches should be encouraged to wait until the new pastor arrives before having their Celebration Sunday and beginning to live together as one church. When churches are ready to merge before a qualified new pastor is available, the roles of pastors from the merging churches must be clearly defined.

Pastors can co-lead successfully if the transition includes pastors clearly defining their respective roles by honoring each other's gifts and skills for ministry. The Crossroads Vital Merger handled the merger of three churches quite well. The three pastors prayed together, engaged in Christian conversation, and decided that one would serve as the Lead Pastor/Administrator, one would serve in overseeing small groups and discipleship, and one would serve primarily in pastoral care. They agreed upon these roles in light of their individual gifts and passions and affirmed each other's ministries. They successfully served the newly merged church for a year until a new pastor arrived.

Good communication between outgoing pastors and the incoming pastor helps the new pastor understand the history of the congregations and the merger process, so he or she can focus on the needs of the new congregation and lead more effectively.

In all Vital Mergers, the Merger Team, as well as all leadership involved, must have a clear understanding of when the merger will occur, when a new pastor will become involved in the merger process, and what the individual roles of pastors will be who serve on interim teams when a new Vital Merger pastor is not available to start on Celebration Sunday.

A Model for Leading

Most mergers have wrestled about whether to retain one or more of the pastors who helped shepherd the churches through the process or to bring in a new pastor to lead the newly merged church. Some questions that arise are: If the new church retains one pastor, which one will they choose? Why will they choose him or her? With some Vital Mergers where one church has a full-time pastor and the other churches have retired or student pastors serving part time, keeping the full-time pastor seems to make sense. However, a pastor's knowledge, gifts, and skills for leading a new church must be assessed and considered when choosing clergy leadership for the Vital Merger.

Pastors who have been assessed and trained as church planters and who have worked with their church through the merger process have a great deal of passion and are invested in the vision of the new church. They are a great asset to the merger process, and many feel that they should have the opportunity to lead the newly merged church. However, retaining one of the current pastors can be problematic because this may create some feeling of ownership on the part of the church that got to keep their own pastor, as well as jealousy from the other churches that lost their pastor.

The Vine, which was a Vital Merger of Peace Church and Grace Church, is a good example. Pastor Elizabeth became lead pastor of The Vine after being pastor of Peace Church before the merger. When she was retained as the pastor of the Vital Merger, some of the people from the Peace Church believed that she had deserted them and preferred the Grace Church congregation. The people from Grace Church felt she was more loyal to the members of the Peace Church. This rift and lack of trust permeated many of their discussions and hindered the church from unifying.

The story of Moses and Joshua provides a model for those planning for leadership transition:

One day the Lord said to Moses, 'Climb one of the mountains east of the river, and look out over the land I have given the people of Israel. After you have seen it, you will die like your brother, Aaron, for you both rebelled against my instructions in the wilderness of Zin. When the people of Israel rebelled, you failed to demonstrate my holiness to them at the waters.' (These are the waters of Meribah at Kadesh in the wilderness of Zin.)

Then Moses said to the Lord, 'O Lord, you are the God who gives breath to all creatures. Please appoint a new man as leader for the community. Give them someone who will guide them wherever they go and will lead them into battle, so the community of the Lord will not be like sheep without a shepherd.'

The Lord replied, "Take Joshua son of Nun, who has the Spirit in him, and lay your hands on him. Present him to Eleazar the priest before the whole community, and publicly commission him to lead the people. Transfer some of your authority to him so the whole community of Israel will obey him.

Numbers 27:12-20 NLT

Moses was the liberator, leading the people out of bondage (the old ways of living together as God's people) and through the wilderness (a place of transition). However, Moses did not take them into the Promised Land. God appointed Joshua, a new leader with new vision and fresh passion, who would help them conquer the enemies that were waiting for them. Joshua had the support of Moses, and understood from Moses that he was to take possession and inhabit the land. Joshua then became accountable to God as he followed God's guidance and led the people into the Promised Land.

Like Moses, pastors have led their churches through the merger process (the transition). They have cast vision and led the people to be faithful to God's guidance. Like Joshua, the new start pastor who leads the people from Celebration Sunday forward will flesh out the vision, define the leadership structure, and help form the churches into one unified church. The new pastor will guide the church as they find, purchase, and move to a permanent location and will help the people identify and form the DNA/core values of the new church.

Passing the leadership baton is not easy. One of the faithful, effective pastors (a Moses), who was instrumental in helping Fellowship Church merger, stated her opposition to appointing a new pastor (a Joshua):

> I'm still a firm believer that it is a huge mistake to remove all clergy who participated and replace them with someone who has not participated in developing the vision. I will always believe this. I don't quite grasp how it is beneficial to remove the person(s) who provide spiritual leadership, who are on board and on the same page with the vision from the beginning and drop in someone with their own agenda and vision on day one. I believe the transition went as smooth as it could have been expected . . ."

While the passion with which this pastor spoke is evident, the fruit the new pastor (the Joshua) and the newly merged church produced was significant. The new church grew by 17 percent over the next three years.

In another Vital Merger, Pastor Alex was the Joshua that led Lakeside Church into the Promised Land. The churches had merged five months before his arrival and were struggling with conflict and jealousy. Alex was able to bring the church together in unity, working with the Location Team in selecting potential sites for the new church, overseeing the capital campaign, working with the Building Committee, shoring up the many teams and committees that existed, hiring additional staff, starting a new worship service, initiating new ministries, marketing the church, and continuing to remind the church that they had become a new entity—a new church.

At the Heritage Vital Merger, the pastor, a Joshua, used his position as the new pastor to help break old traditions. People would sometimes complain to him, "We didn't do it that way at Essex." "We didn't do it that way at Westside." Pastor Michael's mantra was, "I don't know Essex or Westside. I do know Heritage Church, and this is how we do it here."

Assessed and well-trained Joshua's can lead newly merged churches into fruitful ministry. The Vital Mergers where a Joshua has come to lead a new church at the right time (not prematurely to force the merger, and not months after the Celebration Sunday because churches chose to merge prematurely), have grown more quickly and steadily than Vital Mergers where a Moses was retained as Lead Pastor. Where Moses remains to lead the newly merged church, evidence indicates that the congregation will remain at a plateau until the new church moves into a new facility. Once they move into the new facility, they begin to have significant growth.

> ## Think About It
>
> The new Vital Merger pastor needs to be a skilled leader: bringing together the various churches, making disciples of the new people in the church, casting vision for the future, and helping the church live into their new identity.

Regardless of whether the new church is led by a Moses or a Joshua, true Vital Mergers grow (those which adhere to the main commitments outlined in Chapter 1). In contrast, most traditional mergers begin to decline almost immediately. In the mergers where Joshua's have come to lead the new congregations, the churches have experienced steady growth.

Coaching

Just as engaged couples benefit from premarital counseling, having a qualified coach who understands the concepts of church planting is a great asset to any new church start. As soon as a new pastor is appointed or called, a coach works with the pastor and the church through the remainder of the engagement period and at least through the first year of the merger. The coach helps keep the pastor and the church focused on creating a new congregational culture, aligning their ministries with

Leader Tip

Leadership is significant to a successful Vital Merger. A strong lay leadership that works hand in hand with pastoral leadership assures that voices are heard, issues are addressed, dreams are shared, and transitions are made with God's guidance and grace. Good communication between the outgoing pastoral leadership and the new pastor facilitates a transition that honors what was, while moving together into what can be. Outgoing pastors work to prepare the way for the new congregation, and finally, a gifted, assessed, and trained church planter should lead the new congregation into the Promised Land of new ministry together.

their mission, understanding the next important steps to take, and avoiding issues that would derail the project. Securing a church planting coach who is familiar with the Vital Merger process can help the new church avoid some of the landmines that often occur during this period, such as not creating a new community culture soon enough, not reminding the merged church that they are a new church, not focusing on a new mission field, and accepting too many of the traditions of any one of the former churches that merged.

A coach should continue to work with the pastor in the early stages of the Vital Merger. There is much work to be done in integrating the new DNA and core values into the new congregation, developing new ministries and programs, and creating a positive community culture. The coach helps the pastor think through implementing new ideas, provides accountability, and reminds the pastor to care for him/herself.

When churches decide to merge, they enter a time of engagement and transition together. This time is crucial to the success of a Vital Merger. Ideally, a new planting pastor begins meeting with the Merger Team and works with the current pastors to insure a smooth transition. The Merger Team must carefully articulate and lead the churches through the transition process as they anticipate the Celebration Ceremony and future ministry together.

Successful Vital Merger Checklist:

- [ ] Receive a new church-planting pastor. (In the UM church the pastor may be assigned or appointed. In other denominations the pulpit committee will need to begin the search process as soon as possible to call a planting pastor early after the merger is completed.)

The Wedding:
Celebrating the Merger

WEDDINGS ARE A FESTIVE TIME—FULL OF LOVE, HOPE, AND dreams of a happy life together. The wedding is a culmination of time invested in dating and getting to know each other, and months of planning the special event.

The Vital Merger Celebration Sunday is a time of bringing together those churches that have spent months—or years—visioning, planning, and working to make this new church a reality. The Merger Team has spent endless hours discerning a new vision for the church. They have worked hard to draw up the merger document. They have accepted a new pastor, ideally including him or her in planning meetings, and now the new pastor joins them on this very first Sunday together. Celebration Sunday is an exciting event, a rite of passage, the beginning of ministry together as a new church.

Just as a wedding celebration is a gala event that lasts several days with all the showers, rehearsals, and receptions, the Vital Merger Celebration should be a multi-day event. It should include pre-celebrative events, informational meetings, and teams planning various aspects of the celebrations. The celebrations should include parties and get-togethers.

Celebration Sunday itself should be just that—a celebration, an upbeat affair that includes people and groups from every church involved in the merger. The worship service may include choirs from the merging churches as well as newly formed choirs. It may include special liturgy written for the celebration. Depending on the style of worship, the celebration may include a handbell choir, special ensemble, band, drama, poetry slam, multimedia presentation, live testimony or video-taped interview with people from the merging churches.

The Next Steps Church intentionally incorporated people from both of their former churches in their Celebration Sunday worship. They had a combined choir that prepared a special anthem for their Celebration event. Their worship style is more traditional, and during the processional they carried in items that belonged to the former churches such as the pulpit Bible, altar cross, American flag, Christian flag, baptismal font, and communion chalice and paten. They were careful to use an equal number of items representing each church. Their District Superintendent attended and spoke at the celebration. The worship celebration was followed by a dinner and tours of the new building.

Living Hope Church created their Celebration Sunday to be like a wedding ceremony. They celebrated their new life together by saying vows to each other and making a commitment to value each other in this new relationship.

Think About it

The merger celebration should symbolize the beginning of a new future for the new church. Worship should be excellent and celebratory. Special nametags should be used. The church should continue the celebration by eating and fellowshipping together. Special activities should be planned to celebrate the unity of the new church. Gifts or t-shirts with the logo of the new church could be given to each member.

The Celebration Sunday for the Gathering Church included a call to worship that focused on the uniting of the four congregations, and set an evangelistic tone that reflected their mission and vision statements:

We have come together as a new congregation... bringing with us the richness of our heritage as the First, Christ, Grace and Faith[34] congregations. Now we turn our attention outward, to souls who are hungry for Jesus, who have yet to receive the Good News of salvation and who long to have him make a difference in their lives. We are not here for ourselves alone, but for those who are not at the table, and who are yearning for the invitation and for the acceptance that comes with it.

The message that day was entitled "The Gethsemane Moment," which focused on the similarity between Jesus' acceptance of the cross in order to save others and the decision to close four churches in order to better reach those who do not know Jesus.

Each of the Celebration Sunday worship services should include a time of bringing new members into the new church. Until the Celebration Sunday, the new church has no members; all memberships belonged to the merging churches. During their first worship ceremony together, the new church receives all these members as new members. At this time, the new church also receives new members who were not part of the previous churches. In doing so, the church experiences growth from the first Sunday.

Celebration Sunday is a time to kick off a number of new Sunday school classes and small groups. People may assume that they will maintain the "same" classes that they were in before merging. While this provides some continuity, it is better to begin integrating the classes from the first Sunday together. Starting a number of new classes or groups and utilizing new topics for study will help to create a new community culture in the church.

If the merging churches did not already have a strong small group ministry, this is an ideal time to launch this ministry. Strategically starting

Leader Tip

Pastors, don't miss the opportunity to have the congregations exchange vows on Celebration Sunday as you welcome new members.

A Service of Merger of Congregations and Reception of New Members[35]

Pastor to congregation: Friends, we are gathered together in the presence of God to witness and bless the joining together of (*these three congregations*) or (*First Church, Christ Church and Grace Church*) to become a new congregation.

Pastor to leaders of congregation: I ask you now, in the presence of God, to declare your intention to enter into this merger with each other through the grace of Jesus Christ. Do you intend to merge these congregations into a new church, to be known as *New Church?*

Leaders: **We do.**

Pastor: Will you do all in your power to help create a new church that is faithful to Jesus Christ and reaches out in ministry to transform the world?

Leaders: **We will.**

Pastor to the congregation: On behalf of the whole church, I ask you: Do you renounce the spiritual forces of wickedness, reject the evil powers of this world, and repent of your sin?

Congregation responds: **I do.**

Pastor to the congregation: Do you accept the freedom and power God gives you to resist evil, injustice, and oppression in whatever forms they present themselves?

Congregation responds: **I do.**

Pastor to congregation: Do you confess Jesus Christ as your Savior, put your whole trust in his grace, and promise to serve him as your Lord, in union with the church which Christ has opened to people of all ages, nations, and races?

Congregation responds: **I do.**

Pastor to congregation: According to the grace given to you, will you remain a faithful member of Christ's holy church and serve as Christ's representative in the world?

Congregation responds: **I will.**

Pastor to congregation: As a member of Christ's universal church, will you be loyal to this church and do all in your power to strengthen its ministries?

Congregation responds: **I will.**

Pastor to congregation: As a member of this congregation, will you faithfully participate in its ministries?

Congregation responds: **We give thanks for all that God is about to do in this new congregation. As members together in the body of Christ and in this congregation, we renew our covenant to participate in the ministries of the church by our prayers, our presence, our gifts, our service, and our witness, that in everything God may be glorified through Jesus Christ.**

Pastor prays for the congregation. The God of all grace, who has called us to eternal glory in Christ, establish you and strengthen you by the power of the Holy Spirit, that you may live in grace and peace.

Go to www.vitalmerger.com for a free downloadable document.

small groups at this time of transition will help new people get involved in a small group and assist in helping people to build new relationships.

The planning, preparation, and celebration events mark the passage from being single churches to living in ministry together. As part of their celebration, Fellowship Church hosted a series of four weekend Fun Days as a way of celebrating and unifying the congregations. Pastor Tom explained the event:

> *We used a 'seasons' approach and told everyone whose birthday was in the spring to come the first Sunday afternoon of July, summer birthdays would attend the second Sunday afternoon of July, and so forth for fall and winter. Family members got to choose whose birthday would determine which Sunday afternoon they should attend per their own needs and schedules. Some families even chose to attend more than one Fun Day.*
>
> *These Fun Day afternoons were provided by the pastors and staff… and were designed to last one hour.*
>
> *We had fun mixer style games that allowed people to introduce themselves so they could begin getting to know each other. The pastor and staff introduced themselves and anyone could ask anything about them. The staff and pastors pre-planned some questions so that key questions were raised, with some questions being fun, others specifically to cast vision and create community.*

Another church moved into a Big Box store that they leased until their new building was completed. They took possession of the building one week before Celebration Sunday. People came each evening and worked. They built walls, painted, decorated the children's, youth, and worship areas, installed sound and lighting equipment, and got the building ready for their Celebration Sunday. Some of the people met each other for the first time and worked side-by-side, building new friendships.

When Next Steps Church merged, they purchased an abandoned church building in their new mission field (relocating nine miles from the two former churches). People from both churches, now a Vital Merger, spent the day before the Celebration Sunday doing a thorough cleaning of the new church building. The outside landscaping was overgrown, the inside needed cleaning, and many of the rooms needed a fresh coat of paint. At lunchtime they shared a meal together. This clean-up day built community and began long-lasting friendships.

Eating meals together is a great way to build new friendships. Many of the Vital Mergers include a cover-dish or potluck dinner on Celebration Sunday. Some churches have the meals catered so the people can truly focus on celebrating and building relationships rather than cooking and preparing. One church rented a banquet hall and chartered a bus to transport the people to the banquet hall after worship. They wanted people to share transportation as a way of getting to know each other, rather than each driving in their individual cars. They also assigned busses alphabetically according to people's last names to further integrate everyone.

Other churches have planned a church-wide mission project or worked on a Habitat House as a way of celebrating their new life together. As these new members work together they build healthy, new relationships. The Celebration Sunday is the start of a new life together, just like a marriage. It is the joining of churches that previously had their own life, their own mission, and their own traditions, but now form a new life together with a new mission, developing new traditions. From this point on they are united as one church

Successful Vital Merger Checklist

☐ Conduct a final service of celebration of the ministry of each church.

☐ Worship at a neutral location for Celebration Sunday. Hold a celebration worship ceremony with people from each of the merged churches helping to lead their first service as a new church. Begin a new worship service or introduce a new style of worship.

CHAPTER
12

The New Home
for the New Family:
Creating Roots

MOVING IN TOGETHER AFTER THE WEDDING IS AN EXCITING TIME for the newly married couple. Finally, after the waiting period, they have a home and are beginning a new life together. Couples who are blending families know that moving into the homes of one or the other can be problematic. Therefore, couples, who are able, sell their respective homes (if owned) and buy or rent a new home for their new family.

Likewise, the newly merged church ideally moves into their new home on Celebration Sunday where they can begin thriving in their temporary or permanent church home.[36] As with all transitions, along with the excitement comes the need for adjustments. Moving into a neutral location after the merger is probably one of the most controversial decisions during the Vital Merger process, yet also one of the most important. Having a location that is new for everyone minimizes turf issues as well as emphasizes the fact that this is a new church.

Moving to a new location for the first service of the newly merged church is key to the success of the Vital Merger. Some churches navigate this transition more successfully than others. Some develop creative ways of showing people the need for a neutral location.

The Vital Merger Team at Fellowship Church provided a Frequently Asked Questions (FAQ's) sheet to the four congregations and developed a parable to explain the necessity of the neutral location:

Q: *"I still don't understand why we can't move into an existing church and save that money for something else."*

A: *Think of it as a parable of sorts. The four churches (considering the merger) are like an extended family: cousins, aunts, uncles, parents, etc. Suddenly and tragically, one of the churches burns down and now some of our extended family are homeless and without shelter or a place to live. We invite them into our church saying, "Mi casa es su casa. My home is your home. Treat it as your own."*

And for a while we mean that, and they believe it.

But soon the guest family tries to enjoy some of its own traditions or habits and we, the host family say, "Oh, but we don't do it like that here! That is my chair (or pew)." The visiting family does not feel like it is their home despite what we said in our invitation. They feel unwanted and certainly unappreciated. They want a place of their own to call home. They leave, and we are back to our original family unit: elderly, alone, and on our last leg.

Face it; do any of us really want our in-laws or sister with thirteen kids living with us? That is why we need a new church. Everyone starts out on an even basis. We form new ways of doing things; new traditions where everyone feels equal ownership, responsibility, and pride. In a new facility we become a nuclear family, one household.

The argument to move to a temporary, rented facility while the new church owns two, three, or four buildings is often hard for church members to understand. They own their buildings where they can worship and have Sunday school and would not have to set up and tear down every week. However, a neutral location is critical for a Vital Merger's success. The new church home must be home for everyone. Stories of Vital Mergers show that neutrality is necessary.

New Life Church

New Life Church, the first church in the study and development of the Vital Merger model, stayed in the better of their two church buildings. They promised the people that they would buy new land and build a new facility. However, it took ten years to complete the building. During those ten years, there was resentment from many people because the promised facility was delayed. People got discouraged and left. Attendance during those years increased slightly. Once they moved into their new facility, worship attendance increased by 19 percent within the first year.

> ### Think About It
>
> "The attendance has continued to grow during this time, but not as rapidly as it would have if they had been in a common, neutral space for the entire time."
>
> **Pastor Joe,
> New Life Church**

Living Hope Church

Originally, Living Hope made a commitment to stay in one of their buildings until it was sold. They would then use the money from the sale, as well as money from the sale of the other church building and their endowment money, to build their new building. However, the sale of the Christ Church site took longer than anticipated, and the excitement and vision of being a new church in a new facility began to wane. Therefore, they decided to move to a Veterans of Foreign Wars (VFW) hall adjacent to the land upon which they owned

> ### Think About It
>
> "The decision to meet in the Bethel Church building was not productive to unity. Choosing a neutral location did result in better harmony among the members."
>
> **Mary, lay person,
> Living Hope Church**

and planned to build. Moving to a rented facility was a bumpy transition, and some members left. Although the church remained somewhat plateaued during their time in the rented facility, they had less conflict and worked better together as a team. They were unified around the mission and began starting new ministries.

The Connection Church

The Connection chose to remain in the largest building of the three that merged. There were some who wanted to move to the neutral, state-of-the-art high school, but many members and leaders did not see it as a benefit. In this Vital Merger, "Moses" remained as the pastor after the merger. He was a visionary leader and well-loved by the congregations, yet he was not able to leverage the influence necessary to move the congregation to a neutral location at the time of the merger. Once the three churches merged, they filled the sanctuary to 100 percent capacity with standing room only on many Sundays. They were reluctant to begin a second worship service for many of the same reasons that they did not move to a neutral site. Because they had filled the building to capacity, they were not able to increase attendance. When they finally purchased adjacent land, moved the parsonage to a new location, built a new worship center, and converted their old sanctuary into a fellowship hall and additional classrooms, attendance increased rapidly.

Lakeside Church

After Lakeside merged, they began worshipping at one church's facility. This proved problematic since the sanctuary was not handicap accessible, nor was the facility large enough for the congregation to gather for worship. For those who could not access the sanctuary, a "TV Chapel" space was set up where they could watch the service on closed-circuit TV. A few people worshiped in this space, but felt isolated from the congregation. In addition to the sanctuary being inaccessible, most of the building was inaccessible as well. The first Sunday the new pastor led worship at Lakeside, an elderly man fell down the stairs, severely injuring himself. It did not take the people at Lakeside long to begin complaining that the facilities were inadequate. The expected turf issues also arose quickly. They considered moving to one of the other churches that had an elevator, which would alleviate the accessibility issue, but that facility had other disadvantages.

Within a month of the new pastor arriving at Lakeside Church, the people voted to move to an elementary school located within their mission field. This new location provided the needed neutrality for the Vital Merger to be successful as well as an adequate and safe facility. Lakeside Church worshiped in the elementary school for fifteen months. The attendance remained stable during that time. The church sold one of the buildings, retained another building for offices and meeting rooms, and underwent major construction on the third site where they built a 5,000 square foot family life center, renovated existing classrooms into an office complex, remodeled the kitchen, painted all the gathering areas, and turned the old sanctuary into a Heritage Room. In addition, they built a storage barn and completed the site preparation and poured the foundation for their sanctuary. They completed Phase 1 of the project debt-free, using money from endowments and the sale of one of the buildings.

Think About It

"We wish we would not have chosen one of the existing church facilities in which to worship and would have immediately moved worship to the elementary school. This would have eliminated or minimized ownership issues. A neutral site is absolutely the best thing to do and probably one of the best decisions we have made."

**Pastor Alex,
Lakeside Church**

The average worship attendance for the year before they moved into their new building was 165. Their first worship service in their new Family Life Center was held in February, and their first Easter had attendance of 314, with an average attendance in April of that year of 262, including fifty-five first-time guests. Their average worship attendance for the first year was 189 and increased to 217 the following year.

Leader Tip

The real estate adage, "Location, location, location!" is true for churches that want to reach new people. New Life Church purchased fifteen acres of land across the street from a school complex (elementary, middle, and high school) in their mission field. Living Hope purchased ten acres on a busy road leading to the local mall. Fellowship Church is relocating to fifteen acres with high visibility from an interstate highway, a state route, and is on the main road leading to a new high school. Aldersgate Church purchased a closed school building visible from a highly traveled road. Next Steps Church, as previously mentioned, purchased a closed church in a racially mixed neighborhood, becoming the first African American church in that community.

While trying to maintain the spirit of neutrality, some Vital Mergers have decided that the best stewardship, as well as the best location to reach their mission field, is to retain one of the buildings and renovate it extensively. The renovation provides a sense of newness and decreases ownership issues.

Lakeside renovated one of their existing church buildings. After looking at several pieces of property, studying their mission field and their newly-adopted vision, they decided it was best to utilize one of the existing churches. Their rational was solid. They were located in the center of the fastest growing part of their city, adjacent to a new elementary school and across from a busy city park with hundreds of children, young people, and families playing sports. In addition, their property consisted of thirteen acres with great visibility and access.

To create a sense of neutrality and a new church home, they did not use the property for a year. They made major renovations to the existing property and built a new multi-purpose building with a new kitchen.

The old sanctuary would serve as a Heritage Hall through which people would walk to enter the new multi-purpose room and sanctuary. A display representing artifacts and memorials from each of the churches was created in the Heritage Hall. Couches, chairs, and tables were added to this room to create a comfortable and welcoming atmosphere.

Although not all of the Vital Mergers choose to move to a neutral location, it is to their advantage to do so. Creating the sense of neutrality, eliminating ownership issues, and having a new, fully-adequate campus creates opportunities for the new church to flourish and reach more people with the Good News of God's love.

Fellowship Church

The congregations of the Fellowship Vital Merger were very resistant to moving to a new location, partly because two of the outgoing pastors assured the people of their churches that they would not have to move. When the new pastor discovered this, he decided it would cost too much (in people capital and resources) to force a move.

Since they did not move to a neutral location, the pastor insisted that they would not worship in the Calvary Church sanctuary (the largest of the facilities), but would instead worship in Calvary's Fellowship Hall. This would help create a sense of neutrality. Doing so meant setting up every Saturday afternoon and tearing down after worship on Sunday. They also started an additional worship service within a month of the new pastor arriving. To keep the momentum going, they established a Site Committee to look for potential building sites, and purchased land within nine months of the merger. Worship attendance at Fellowship Church has increased 17 percent since the merger.

Next Steps Church

Next Steps Church took the principle of neutrality to heart. In April, they voted to merge on the first Sunday of July. They negotiated with their district to purchase a church building that had been closed a year earlier. They relocated from an urban neighborhood to an inner ring suburb (suburbs that are close to the city).

Next Steps Church left their old buildings on the last Sunday of June and came together as one church the first Sunday of July. They celebrated the unity that had already been forming between the churches as they had met, dreamed, and planned together.

The church started connecting with their new community and attracting new people. They opened their facility to the neighborhood for basketball and hosted a Basketball Camp. They began a tutoring program with the local school and started an Academic Challenge Team to make learning fun for the students. By connecting to the community in these ways, people from the community began attending Next Steps Church.

A strategically chosen neutral location with a suitable facility positions the new church for new growth and opens the door to creative and healthy change.

Successful Vital Merger Checklist

☐ Move into a neutral church home where the new church can thrive.

☐ Carefully choose a strategic location with a suitable facility to position the new church for growth and fruitful ministry.

☐ Develop a marketing plan targeting the new mission field, highlighting the existence of the new church worshipping in a new location.

CHAPTER
13

Keeping the Marriage Alive: Building Unity for a Long Life

A WEDDING CEREMONY LASTS ONLY A FEW MINUTES, BUT COUples hope their marriage will last a lifetime. Joining lives together requires hard work, dedication, determination, and of course, love. Likewise, Vital Mergers require hard work, dedication, love for each other, and openness to God's guidance, which helps the church move into fruitful ministry together. Building unity in the new church is multifaceted and must be intentional. This unity blossoms as a result of creating a new congregational culture, focusing on vision alignment, creating a discipleship process, and developing new ministries that reflect core values of the new church.

Creating a New Congregational Culture

Creating a shared vision and culture draws the newly merged congregation into a sense of togetherness. The sooner the new community culture can be created, the better, because old habits die hard and so do congregational cliques. For example, in one Vital Merger of three churches, several months after the Celebration Sunday, the new pastor noticed that the people were sitting in three different groups that each represented a pre-merger congregation. At that point, he took decisive action to find ways to mix the groups and to do more to build a new congregational culture.

Vital Mergers can create a shared culture in many ways. Pastor Linda of Living Hope Church gave some examples of how Living Hope worked to bring about a new community culture. "Participation in social activities, picnics, Bible studies, fundraising activities, and joint participation in the plans for land procurement and building designs have helped to blend the two congregations," she said. Pastor Joe from New Life Church took people from his new Vital Merger on a mission trip to help create a new culture. Another pastor said that having a Capital Campaign that was focused on raising money for their new building was a significant uniting factor for their church. In another Vital Merger, the congregations began developing a number of new ministries to reach their newly identified mission field. They also worked together with ministries that already existed in the two churches prior to merger in order to build a sense of unity.

Deciding on a new name early in the process can be a significant unifying factor. For this reason, the new name for the church should be included in the merger document. One Vital Merger delayed giving a name to their new church. People reasoned that they should wait until the church had a clear vision and time to live out the new DNA before they could give a name reflecting the church's new identity. However, because the new church had no name, the people did not see it as a new church or as ministry together. As a result, it began taking on the characteristics of a traditional merger. The lack of a name became a divisive issue rather than a unifying factor. Nine months after the merger celebration, the church finally voted on a new name.

Pastor Alex at Lakeside Church found that moving to a neutral worship site helped to create the new congregational culture. The church had initially resisted moving to a neutral site, stating that they owned three church buildings. They could save money by avoiding a rent payment and reasoned that they would feel more at home in one of their own buildings. When warned that this would result in jealousy and hard feelings, they insisted that this would not happen with them. Within weeks of worshipping together they were already arguing about using one of the other buildings. When they moved to an elementary school for Sunday worship, they began uniting as one congregation.

In an attempt to create a new congregational culture, Pastor Alex continued to hold town hall style meetings after the Celebration Sunday. He hosted monthly congregational meetings, usually led by the original Merger Team, to continue to communicate decisions and direction. This provided an open forum for asking questions and for church leadership to provide transparency. It also gave Alex a monthly platform for vision casting.

Pastor Joe at New Life Church provided a Lenten Devotional Guide from stories contributed by longtime participants in the two congregations. The devotional offered an opportunity for people at New Life Church to become acquainted with the stories of others in their new church. By understanding and gaining respect for each other through hearing these faith stories, they experienced a sense of unity from which they could create a shared congregational culture.

Pastor Jason at the Gathering Church credits the new, healthy community culture to their focus on the new mission and vision of the church. "We talk about how well we are working on our mission and vision, and how we've been able to identify, invite, and involve new people, as well as having an impact on the community. We've gained a reputation as 'a praying church' given the way we've surrounded all our work with prayer." The church constructed a Prayer Wall in their new building modeled after Jerusalem's Western Wall. People from the church and the community fill the cracks between the stones of the wall with their written prayer concerns.

Focusing on Vision Alignment

As people in the new church focus together on shared vision, they will experience a sense of oneness and begin to form a new church culture guided by that vision. This vision must be clearly articulated and all ministries in the new church must be aligned with the vision. In a Vital Merger, as with any new church, if the vision of ministry is not clearly articulated, some people might focus on a short-term vision such as building a new building so they can move out of the neutral worship space. The vision of the new church must be more comprehensive and far reaching than buying or building a new facility, though the vision can and should direct the design and use of that facility.

For example, New Life Church initially developed a vision to reach the people in their community who were either unchurched or de-churched by telling them about the love of Jesus. The pastor constantly cast this vision to the congregation. As a result, they designed a facility to reach the people of the community through childcare, mentoring, youth activities, partnering with the YMCA, operating a coffee shop, and having open meeting spaces for a variety of groups, both Christian and social agencies. In fact, Pastor Joe says:

> *There really were no significant changes made to the vision, because the vision was not on merging the churches, or building a new facility or relocation. All of those were just means to reach our community for Christ. I believe we have been able to come this far because our vision was focused on reaching our community for Christ.*

Lakeside Church had an effective vision that focused on uniting its congregation while reaching new people for Christ. They initiated a number of short-term goals to accomplish their long-term vision, including: relocating to a growing part of town, building a new building which included a family life center and a dedicated sanctuary, and initiating new programs and ministries to reach the unchurched. These goals were short-term, focusing on accomplishing them within the first five years of being a new church.

Three years into the merger, the church had accomplished most of these goals. In addition, they started a new alternative worship service, started a number of small groups, and provided many fellowship and service opportunities for the new church. Because they had accomplished most of their goals, they developed a new Vision Team to begin looking toward the future. This provided an opportunity for the new pastor to have a significant impact on the direction of the church, to further develop the DNA, and direct the church's focus on important ministries.

The Gathering Church adopted mission and vision statements with a focus on evangelism that has kept the congregation excited and motivated. They found out through research that more than 14,000 people within a four-mile radius of the church had no religious affiliation. The church focused their ministry on inviting these 14,000 people to experience a new relationship with Christ. As the people of the church say it, "We want them to feel like they've gone to heaven before they died."

As the new church sells its old building, purchases land, and builds a new building, it is easy for the people to become so excited about the building and so focused on moving out of their neutral location, that they lose sight of the actual vision. Pastor Betsy, from Living Hope, observes: "Just because a church stays together does not mean they have caught the vision. Much focus and attention was placed on building the new building. Now that it is completed we are working on finding our new identity in Christ."

Establishing a Discipleship Process

Every church needs a discipleship process. A discipleship process helps people move from curiosity to commitment as they grow in their faith. A clearly defined discipleship process builds unity in a Vital Merger as people from different places in their spiritual journey come together to learn and invite new Christians into a life of discipleship.

The discipleship process provides a primary method to instill new core values into the new church. Outlining a clear path for discipleship that is consistent with the new core values will produce disciples that

Leader Tip

Successful Vital Mergers are measured by distinctive characteristics:

- The Vital Merger has a unified sense of mission and vision
- Three years after the merger, people in the congregation refer to the church by the merged name instead of identifying themselves with their pre-merged church
- Three years after the merger, the congregation is larger than the average worship attendance of the pre-merged churches
- Three years after the merger, the congregation is in a better financial position than the pre-merged churches
- By year five after the merger, at least 40 percent of the congregation is new since the merger.

have a strong value for what they are taught. For example, at Fellowship Church, Pastor Tom wanted to make sure that the church would be known for its effective small groups and missions. The newly merged church started a number of small groups right away, and required that everyone with leadership responsibilities must be in a small group. Going forward, all leaders were chosen from those active in a small group. In addition, Fellowship Church developed a number of mission areas in which people could serve God, trained people to be focused on mission in their community and beyond, and sponsored numerous mission trips.

The New Life Vital Merger provides another example for the need for a discipleship process. The new people this church attracted needed a way to understand the church, its mission, and vision, as well as what it meant to be a Christian. Pastor Joe said, "Whether they were formerly churched or not, they seemed to be locked into a consumerist paradigm of congregational involvement. We needed to engage a process to convert them to a discipleship orientation."

Therefore, the discipleship process for New Life Church begins with inviting new people into a small group, and then urges them to make a commitment to a two-year Christian training process. During this process they discover ways to be involved in the life of the church and use their gifts for ministry in the community.

Developing New Ministries that Reflect New Core Values

Beginning new ministries builds unity as people look to their future and work in ministry together. A foundational core value upon which all new ministries must be built is "making disciples of Jesus Christ for the transformation of the world."[37] Developing ministries needed for this mission and tailoring ministries to reach new people unites the newly merged church around new core values.

Living Hope Church developed ministries that reach their mission field. Because their community was facing economic struggles, they utilized their building to offer hospitality to the community by becoming a distributor of Angel Food Ministries in their area. They also partnered with AARP to offer tax preparation for seniors. As people come to the church, they are greeted by church members who offer them coffee, tea, and other snacks. The church's Prayer Room is open to everyone, and members are available to pray with people.

One of the core values of New Life Church is showing hospitality to its local community. New Life, located in a rural area, partnered with the YMCA to provide services to the local residents by inviting children and adults to use the gymnasium in their new building. Another way they showed hospitality was hosting an After Prom party for the local school.

These ministries are not unique since many existing churches do similar ministries. However, these ministries are often new to those coming together as a new church with new core values based on discipleship and witness.

The stories and steps outlined in this book are shared with hope that more people will seriously consider creating new places for new people through the Vital Merger process. Vital Merger ministry is an invitation to churches to come together with other churches as a new church and walk with Jesus in more dedicated and effective discipleship and witness. Healthy, fruitful, vital congregations will reach more people with hope and the saving love of Jesus Christ so that the world is transformed.

For many churches joining together in a Vital Merger, the process is more than just merging. It is a time of renewal as the churches reconnect with Jesus and discover their first love again.

APPENDIX 1:
Checklist for a Successful Vital Merger Process

- [ ] Establish a prayer team with representatives from each church.
- [ ] Saturate the entire merger process in prayer and seek God's direction as everyone moves forward.
- [ ] Contact a judicatory official (if applicable) when prayer team discerns the direction to proceed with a merger.
- [ ] The judicatory official establishes a date for an initial meeting with key leadership from all churches. The judicatory staff person responsible for church planting should be included in this initial meeting.
- [ ] Each church's Council or Board votes to be involved in the merger talks.
- [ ] Establish a Merger Team to discuss merger issues, with equal representation from each church. Divide the Merger Team into two sub-teams:
  - an Administrative Team to focus on the logistics and legalities of the merger, and
  - a Vision Team to focus on the mission, vision and programs of the future church. This team is tasked with answering
- [ ] Merger Team completes a demographic study for the existing church communities and for potential relocation sites.
- [ ] Vision Team answers three questions:
  - What is God's vision for our community?
  - How can we best reach more people with God's message of love?
  - What can we do better together than we can do separately?
- [ ] Create numerous opportunities for both congregations to get to know each other.

Go to www.vitalmerger.com for a free downloadable document.

- Organize joint worship experiences, celebration events, and opportunities unrelated to the discussion of the proposed merger.
- Provide a variety of small group opportunities.
- Alternate worshipping sites to become familiar with each other and gain an appreciation for the ministries and setting of each church.

☐ Establish communication channels and processes to maintain regular communication from the Merger Team to all the churches involved in the merger talks. Communication is best accomplished when Merger Team communiqué is presented to each church by the representatives from their respective churches.

☐ Conduct periodic "straw polls" to assure that each church is still on-board with the idea of a merger.

☐ Make adjustments in communications channels to address issues that arise.

☐ Develop a "merger document" that outlines the details of the new church. The merger document should include:
- Brief History and Future Intent
- New Mission Statement
- Definition of the Mission Field
- New name
- Timeline and Process
- Leadership Structure
- Personnel/Staffing
- Property, Buildings, Location, and Artifacts
- Rationale for worshipping in a neutral location
- Financial Assets
- Resolution of acceptance and Intent
  - Outlining who may vote
  - Outlining the percentage of vote required for passage
  - Defining number of churches needed for merger to be approved
- Certified Resolution

☐ Send a copy of each draft of the merger document to the appropriate judicatory official and staff person responsible for church planting.

☐ Hold town hall style meetings to inform all congregations of the progress of the merger document and to answer questions concerning the future of the church.

☐ Have an attorney review the merger document for legal purposes.

☐ Forward the completed merger document to appropriate judicatory officials.

☐ Make the completed copy of the merger document available to members of each church for study and discussion.

☐ Contact a judicatory official (if applicable) to authorize a church conference or congregational meeting for the "Merger Vote."

☐ Define and communicate who is eligible to vote before the meeting. Review records and remove those who are ineligible to vote BEFORE taking the vote. Each tribe may have different rules. For example, in a United Methodist Church/Charge Conference the following people have a vote:
  • Professing members (those who have taken membership as professions of faith or by transfer)
  • Retired Ministers and Diaconal Ministers who hold their charge conference membership at the church
  • Affiliate Members[38]

☐ Take the vote. Set the bar for approval at two-thirds (66%) of those voting to insure that a larger percentage of the congregation is in support of the merger[39].

Once the merger has been accepted:

☐ Take care of legal/logistical matters. Begin the process of incorporating, gaining new postal permits, selling buildings, and purchasing a new facility or site for construction of a new building.

☐ Receive a new church-planting pastor. (In the UM church the pastor may be assigned or appointed. In other denominations the pulpit committee will need to begin the search process as soon as possible to call a planting pastor early after the merger is completed.)

☐ Carefully choose a strategic location with a suitable facility to position the new church for growth and fruitful ministry.

☐ Conduct a final service of celebration of the ministry of each church.

☐ Worship at a neutral location for Celebration Sunday. Hold a celebration that includes people from each of the merged churches for the first service together. This is a great time to begin a new worship service or introduce a new style of worship.

☐ Move into a neutral church home where the new church can thrive.

☐ Develop a marketing plan targeting the new mission field, highlighting the existence of the new church worshipping in a new location.

Churches that complete the entire checklist create a healthy new church that effectively reaches the community with the Good News of Jesus Christ. Each step helps negotiate the difficulties of the merging process in ways that will minimize the stress and grief, while positioning the new church for future growth.

APPENDIX 2:
Sample Merger Document

First, Christ, and Grace Churches Becoming New Church UMC

MERGER RESOLUTION

We, the Board of Trustees of First UMC, Christ UMC, and Grace UMC, of Anytown, Anystate, being Anystate Ecclesiastical Corporations, at separately held meetings on April 15, 2013, hereby resolve to merge into one church called New Church as of July 1, 2013 for the purposes and on the terms and conditions set forth below. We request that this merger resolution be approved at an officially scheduled Church Conference of our churches and by our District Superintendent as provided for in the 2012 Book of Discipline of the United Methodist Church, Part V, Chapter 6, paragraph 2546.

ITEM 1: THE PURPOSE OF THE MERGER

The congregations of First United Methodist Church, Christ United Methodist Church, and Grace United Methodist Church have been faithfully serving the Anytown, Anystate community for many decades. They have brought the message of Jesus Christ to many in their existence and it is the desire to be more effective at this task that has drawn us to the vision of this church merger, becoming a new church start. The churches understand the need to be more effective in making and maturing disciples of Jesus Christ as the number of unchurched people grows in our community and nation. With that thought in mind we have prayerfully pursued God's vision for the church in our community.

It is our belief that in combining the many gifts and talents in our individual churches, we will be better equipped to face the opportunities ahead. It is our intent to enter into a Vital Church Merger, a merger

Go to www.vitalmerger.com for a free downloadable document.

of the congregations into one church, creating a new place to worship, combining all assets, resetting the new congregation's focus on the mission field, beginning new ministries that will reach this new mission field, and choosing a new name which is not a part of the name of any of the churches merging. In line with the definition of a Vital Church Merger, we will combine our membership, assets, and resources to multiply our energy and programs to create a new fellowship of believers: New Church UMC. With the establishment of New Church UMC, we begin the process of finding or building a new worship facility. It is our desire that New Church UMC be a place where people come to experience the love of Jesus Christ through our message and our actions. As we search scripture and look at our present church bodies as well as the community around us, we feel led to unite as one church to meet the need of our community.

My prayer is not for them alone. I pray also for those who will believe in me through their message, that all of them may be one, Father, just as you are in me and I am in you. May they also be in us so that the world may believe that you have sent me. I have given them the glory that you gave me, that they may be one as we are one: I in them and you in me. May they be brought to complete unity to let the world know that you sent me and have loved them even as you have loved me. John 17:20-23

We will also persist in prayer as we move forward with the vision.

Do not be anxious about anything, but in everything, by prayer and petition, with thanksgiving, present your requests to God. Philippians 4:6

The merger of these three congregations will fill a great need. All three churches are stepping out in faith with a great deal of courage and a willingness to sacrifice. None of us is sure of the results of this endeavor, but all three feel the call of God to build a new house of worship. Our church conference vote will indicate that a vote in favor of creating the new church means that we are willing to leave our current church locations. The final decision on location will be made and voted on pending review of available locations. Prayer will be our constant guide as we listen to God's direction.

ITEM 2: NEW CHURCH NAME

As a result of Visioning Committee meetings, with both churches represented, several names for the new church were presented to all congregations for consideration. Following several weeks of discernment, a ballot vote was taken at each church. This powerful scripture, in which the Bible states, ". . . *select an appropriate scripture* . . . ." This passage serves as the inspiration and positive motivator for choosing **New Church United Methodist Church** as the new name. As we begin the journey as New Church UMC, we can build a church of people going forward to make and grow disciples of Christ.

ITEM 3: MISSION STATEMENT

"Make Disciples of Jesus Christ for the Transformation of the World"

ITEM 4: PROGRAMS AND MINISTRIES

Programs are essential to maintain and develop existing members and attract new members. These programs must nurture the congregation, provide opportunities for outreach, and allow occasions where witness is embraced. The New Church Lead Team will evaluate all nurture, outreach, and witness programs of the churches that were in effect prior to the creation of New Church. The Lead Team will then develop unified programs for New Church that are consistent with the mission and vision statements of the church.

ITEM 5: STRUCTURE

Immediately upon final approval of this merger resolution, a Transition Nominating Committee shall be established including the pastors as co-chairpersons and two representatives from each church. The Transition

Nominating Committee will nominate a Lead Team or Church Council, as well as the names of the persons for approval for all committees of the church. During the first year of operation of the new church, each participating church will have as equal representation to the extent possible on all decision-making bodies. The Transition Nominating Committee shall then be dissolved.

The New Church Lead Team will conform to and comply with the *Book of Discipline of the United Methodist Church* and have full governing authority over all programs, facilities, and local church ministries. The new church will be considered "chartered" the date the merger is official.

The New Church UMC structure is encouraged to be as simple and as lean as possible. This will include a minimal number of committees or teams, with each focused on carrying out the Mission of the church as their primary objective.

The structure, composition of, and duties/responsibilities of all committees will follow the guidelines as set forth in *The BOOK of DISCIPLINE*, Part VI, Organization and Administration, The Local Church, ¶243-259. The final form of the local church structure will be coordinated and voted upon within one year of the merger.

Every attempt shall be made to include on each committee all segments of the congregation. Additionally, it is recommended that no officer/chairperson serve more than three (3) consecutive years in the same office. All committee members shall be members of the church unless permitted to be non-members by *The BOOK of DISCIPLINE*.

The members present and voting at any duly announced meeting shall constitute a *quorum*. (¶252.6)

ITEM 6: PERSONNEL

It is understood that one of the requirements of the Vital Merger is that none of the pastors from the merging churches will remain at the merged church, and the church will receive a pastor that has been assessed and trained as a church planter to lead the church into the future.

The following positions shall be filled by salaried or hourly paid positions, or dedicated unpaid staff: pastor(s), accompanist/organist(s), music director, contemporary worship leader, secretary(ies), and custodian(s), nursery worker(s), children's coordinator, and other positions as determined by the Lead Team. No current employee of any of the churches is guaranteed employment. All positions will be posted and an interview process will be conducted for each position.

ITEM 7: PROPERTY, BUILDING(S), LOCATION, AND ARTIFACTS

Upon the approval of the Vital Merger, the location for the temporary place of worship must be determined.

The Lead Team of New Church UMC shall create a Location Team. The Location Team will determine the most appropriate sites for temporary and permanent worship. They will also make recommendations and arrangements for the possible use or sale of surplus facilities and properties.

The Location Team shall identify and present all temporary worship locations to the Lead Team. The Lead Team will present the recommendations to the newly merged church for discussion on the decision on the temporary worship site.

The Location Team will begin to evaluate all things associated with a new permanent worship center. These considerations will include location, necessary inclusions such as building a new facility or remodeling an existing one, square footage, construction type and materials, needs of worship space, office space, child care programs, storage, parking, site access and visibility, costs, financing, etc.

As important as locations are, it will be the Mission Field (community) that drives our new ministry – how to reach more people for Jesus Christ. The Location Team shall solicit advice and obtain the approval of the District Committee on Buildings and Location and the District Superintendent. The Locations Team will evaluate all aspects associated with a new permanent worship center. These considerations will include location, necessary inclusions such as building a new facility or remodeling an existing one, square footage, construction type and materials, needs of worship space, office space, child care programs, storage, parking, site access and visibility, costs, financing, etc.

Upon the effective date of this merger, all real property owned by First UMC, Christ UMC, and Grace UMC, including the church buildings and surrounding land shall be continued to be owned by it under its new name, New Church UMC.

Parsonages: Upon the effective date of this merger, the parsonages owned by First UMC, Christ UMC, and Grace UMC shall be conveyed to New Church UMC.

Following the approval of the Vital Merger, the Trustees of the participating churches will conduct a thorough inventory of each congregation's various properties and assets. In conducting this inventory, the Trustees will use the following definition of "Artifact" when making their determinations of what is to be included on their inventory lists.

Artifact - Any object made by human hands and synonymous with the associated terms of: relic, mementos, remembrance, souvenir, token and vestige.

The Trustees will make a list of all items determined to be included in these categories. All such artifacts/memorials that have been given to each church will remain the sole property of those churches. They may be sold, given to the appropriate person/place, disposed of, or maintained at the discretion of each church. Any funds raised through the sale of any such items will be placed into the building fund of New Church UMC.

All reasonable efforts will be made to notify families that have made tangible memorials in order to determine their wishes for the disposition of such items that are not being retained by the new church. The manner of notification may include phone, mail, or announcements from the pulpit, in newsletters, or in bulletins.

The Trustees shall record how items are dispersed.

All permanent records and archives such as membership, baptismal, marriage, death/funeral, and historical information from all churches will be maintained, appropriately boxed to ensure safekeeping and preservation and will be taken to a central, secure location for safekeeping.

The Trustees will evaluate the parsonages available and recommend to the Lead Team which parsonage(s) will be retained and which will be sold.

ITEM 8: FINANCIAL ASSETS AND LIABILITIES

Upon the effective date of this merger, all assets and liabilities of each church will become assets and liabilities of New Church UMC. The utmost care will be taken to ensure the proper use of all transferred assets that have a designated or restricted use. As soon as is feasible, the newly merged church will become incorporated.

ITEM 9: TIMELINE

The newly merged church, if accepted, will unite on the first Sunday of July. The period of time between the acceptance and the uniting celebration will be a time of preparation for the merger. Each church will maintain its current status, including worship, until the merger is completed.

APPROVAL OF MERGER RESOLUTION

Prior to the date of the Called Church Conference for all churches involved in the merger conversation, acting on behalf of, and at the request of the Merger Team, all legal documents relative to this proposed merger shall have been vetted and approved by certified legal counsel and presented to all congregations and to the District Superintendent.

WHEREAS:

The merging churches formed a merger committee comprised of three (3) members and the pastor from each church, which has met and determined that a merger on the terms and conditions set forth in this MERGER DOCUMENT will more effectively fulfill their ministries, and;

This MERGER DOCUMENT was prepared with the use of *The BOOK of DISCIPLINE OF THE UNITED METHODIST CHURCH* as the guide for procedures and was adopted by each Board of Trustees, and;

The MERGER DOCUMENT and its terms and conditions were presented and proposed to an officially called Church Conference of each of the merging chufches on April 15, 2013, and;

All of the terms and conditions of the MERGER DOCUMENT were approved and authorized by a two-thirds vote of the professing members present at each church conference,

THEREFORE:

This MERGER DOCUMENT does fairly and with all good faith and knowledge represent the terms and conditions that begin the establishment of New Church.

FURTHERMORE:

Said MERGER DOCUMENT does cover nine(9) items: Purpose, Naming, Mission Statement, Programs and Ministries, Structure, Leadership, Property Concerns, Financial Assets and Liabilities, and Timeline.

NOW :

Presents to the Bishop of the North Conference and the Cabinet for approval.

SIGNATURES OF OFFICERS:

_____   _____
Presiding Chairperson   Presiding Chairperson
First UMC Board of Trustee   Christ UMC Board of Trustee

_____   _____
Presiding Chairperson
Grace UMC Board of Trustee

MERGER APPROVAL OF DISTRICT SUPERINTENDENT

This joint resolution for the merger of First UMC, Christ UMC, and Grace UMC, having complied with the 2012 Book of Discipline of the United Methodist Church is hereby approved.

Date: _____   _____

District Superintendent

APPENDIX 3:
Sample Straw Poll Ballot

STRAW POLL SUNDAY!

(Responses are anonymous!)

WHAT THIS IS ABOUT: Two weeks ago today, the Merger Teams in all of the three churches (First, Grace, and Christ) presented their teams' recommendations to the respective congregations.

After over a year of study, evaluation, and prayer, the Merger Team has recommended a Vital Merger. A Vital Merger is the combining of all three existing churches into one new church with a new structure and identity. The team considered "yoking" of churches, shared ministries, shared staff, combining into an existing church, etc. Our studies and work leave us no doubt that a Vital Merger is the best way to utilize all of the resources from all the churches. And most importantly, each member would feel as if the new church was their own.

It is our firm and unanimous belief that a merger of this type is the best way to fulfill our obligation to those who have gone before us, those future generations, and most importantly, to bring disciples to Jesus Christ.

WHAT THIS IS:

This is a request for your input. We need to know how you feel about a Vital Merger. It provides a chance for you to express **your feelings and opinions**, either for or against.

We ask that you take a moment to complete the poll. Please include any remarks, for or against, that you would like to share. If against the merger, please indicate why and feel free to use the back if needed!

Go to www.vitalmerger.com for a free downloadable document.

_____

_____ Yes! I can embrace the vision of the Merger Team
_____ No! I cannot embrace the vision of the Merger Team

Would you participate if the Merger becomes a reality?
_____ Yes   _____ No

(Comments or Questions:) _____

_____

I am a: Church member_____, Attendee_____, Youth_____

All are welcomed and encouraged to respond!

APPENDIX 4:
Sample Ballot

NEW CHURCH/VITAL MERGER INITIATIVE

A. The Vital Merger Team, after prayer and discernment from God, believes it is the best course for the each of the churches to become a new church. They have provided a merger document to outline the rationale, steps, and decisions.

B. The purpose of this Church Conference is to vote on the creation of a new church. A "yes" vote indicates that you are in favor of creating the new church, that you have studied the merger document, and you are in basic agreement with this direction.

C. Immediately upon a ⅔ vote of the members of each church to create the new church, the new Church Council will be created. During the first two years of operation of the new church, each participating church will have as equal representation as possible on the Church Council. The new Church Council will have full governing authority over all programs and facilities.

D. The effective date of the merger will be July 1 of the following year. Commencing on that date, the new church will meet at a neutral location for worship. No ministry programs will be held at any of the previous church buildings.

E. The new Church Council will immediately create a Location Committee to evaluate possible permanent locations for the new church. Each participating church will have two members on the Location Committee. The Location Committee shall, by at least a ¼ vote, present their suggested location for a vote by all members of the new church within one year. The Location Committee will consult with the District Committee on Buildings and Location. The Location Committee may recommend no more than two possible

Go to www.vitalmerger.com for a free downloadable document.

sites. A simple majority vote of church members present at a church conference will be required to approve the location decision.

F. The new Church Council will evaluate all outreach and other programs of the churches that were in effect prior to the creation of the new church. The council will then develop a unified program for the new church that is consistent with the mission and vision statements of the new church.

___ Yes, I am in favor of this proposal.

___ No, I am opposed to this proposal.

APPENDIX 5:
Characteristics of Vital Merger Planting Pastors

It takes a particular type of pastor to lead a Vital Merger post-merger. What are the qualities and characteristics needed for this type of ministry?

First, recognizing that this is a new church start, the pastor would need to be gifted with church planter qualities. This pastor needs to have a desire to reach new people, help the church recognize their new DNA/core values, formulate and oversee new ministries, and help to create a united community of faith. It's also important for the pastor to support those going through the grief of missing their former church, care for the pastoral needs of the people, and guard against the desire of many to return to the status quo of their former church. In addition, the new pastor will lead the church into a new facility, possibly buying land, designing the facility, and raising the money for the new building. It is important that the new pastor go through a formal assessment process to ensure that he or she is indeed a church planter.[40]

The following are some of the qualities and characteristics of Vital Merger church planters.[41]

1. They demonstrate a vibrant faith.
2. They are self-aware and have a coachable spirit.
3. They are innovative and entrepreneurial.
4. They have a history of leading/participating in at least one vibrant, growing church, preferably in a previously healthy new church start.
5. They have a significant experience of God that drives them to want to reach new people.
6. They have demonstrated a history of building relationships in the community and leading their friends into church life.
7. They have affinity for the mission field.

8. They (and their spouse) agree to embrace the sacrifices entailed in the ministry of new church development.
9. They have good listening skills and a compassionate spirit, able to give assurance and help merging churches through the tender feelings and transition issues of letting go of the old and embracing the new.
10. They are competent vision-casters, able to cast vision and move the Vital Merger into becoming a growing, healthy new church start.

Endnotes

1. "A Sneak Peek at Research on Church Mergers," *Church Smart Magazine*, April, 2011.
2. Jim Tomberlin and Warren Bird. *Better Together: Making Church Mergers Work* (San Francisco: Jossey-Bass, 2012), 21.
3. Jim Tomberlin and Warren Bird. *Better Together: Making Church Mergers Work* (San Francisco: Jossey-Bass, 2012), 27-29.
4. Jim Tomberlin and Warren Bird. *Better Together: Making Church Mergers Work* (San Francisco: Jossey-Bass, 2012), 103.
5. C. Peter Wagner, *Church Planting For a Greater Harvest* (California: Regal Books, 1990), 7.
6. Glen Rediehs and Larry Webb, *Healthy Church DNA* (New York: iUniverse, Inc., 2008), 58.
7. Wikipedia contributors, "DNA," *Wikipedia, The Free Encyclopedia*. Wikipedia, The Free Encyclopedia, July 11,2012, http://en.wikipedia.org/wiki/Dna.
8. Tom Bandy, "Missional Mergers: 9 Keys to Success," *Outreach Magazine*, May/June, 2009.
9. Many resources are available about incorporating the discipline of prayer within a church, such as: Cheryl Sacks, *The Prayer-Saturated Church: A Comprehensive Handbook for Prayer Leaders.*Colorado: NavPress, 2007.
   Daniel Henderson and Jim Cymbala, *Transforming Prayer: How Everything Changes When You Seek God's Face.*Minnesota: Bethany House Publisher, 2011.
10. Terry Teykl, *Pray the Price* (Indiana: Prayer Point Press, 1997), 10.
11. Thanks to The Gathering Church for this great idea.
12. Richard J Foster, *Prayer: Finding the Heart's True Home*. New York: HarperCollins, 1992.
13. Ebenezer means "The stone of help." See 1 Samuel 4-7.
14. For a more complete explanation of Prayer Walking read *Prayerwalking: Praying On Site with Insight*, by Steve Hawthorne and Graham Kendrick. Florida: Charisma House Publishers, 1993.
15. Susan Gregory, *The Daniel Fast: Feed Your Soul, Strengthen Your Spirit, and Renew Your Body*. Illinois: Tyndale Momentum, 2010.
16. See Appendix 1 for complete list of steps
17. Jim Collins, *Good to Great*, (New York: Harper Collins Publisher, 2001),13.
18. ¶247.2, *The Book of Discipline of the United Methodist Church*, (Tennessee: United Methodist Publishing House, 2012), 171.
19. The official book on polity of The United Methodist Church
20. Luke 9:49-50

21. Evangelical Lutheran Church in America, "Commonly Asked Questions" on Stewardship, http://www.elca.org/Growing-In-Faith/Discipleship/Stewardship/Stewardship-Key-Leader/Questions.aspx.

22. James D. Klote & Associates, http://www.jdklote.com/services/articles/best-church-capital-campaign-management-company

23. The Free Dictionary by Farlex. http://legal-dictionary.thefreedictionary.com/prenuptial+agreement.

24. In the polity of the United Methodist Church, all members are voting members in major directional decisions of the congregation.

25. The Book of Discipline of the United Methodist Church, ¶228.2b1

26. In the United Methodist Church any member has the right to vote on all-church decisions such as a merger. They must be present to vote. ¶248. In addition, removing inactive members requires a two-year process. ¶228.2b.1

27. Those who hold membership at another UM church, but have taken affiliate membership at any of the churches considering merger.

28. (Although the UM Book of Discipline requires only a simple majority for the merger to take place, it is strongly recommended that a standard of 2/3 majority be required for passage).

29. One of the best books on the subject of transition is: William Bridges. *Managing Transitions: Making the Most of Change*, 3rd ed. Philadelphia: Da Capo Press, 2009.

30. For a more detailed description of a simplified structure, see: John Edmund Kaiser. *Winning On Purpose: How To Organize Congregations to Succeed in Their Mission.* Tennessee: Abingdon, 2006.

31. In United Methodist Churches this is generally the Staff Parish Relations Committee.

32. For United Methodist churches the church needs to be assigned a new GCFA number.

33. In an appointive system like the United Methodist Church, these issues could have been resolved before the merger took place. Ideally, the merger should be effective on July 1, or the date clergy assignments begin.

34. As with all the church names listed, these are not the actual names of the churches involved in this merger.

35. Adapted from the United Methodist Book of Worship (Tennessee: The United Methodist Publishing House, 1992), 88-94, 116-118.

36. Some churches are able, in coordination with the new pastor, to procure a permanent facility immediately.

37. The Mission Statement of the United Methodist Church

38. Those who hold membership at another UM church, but have taken affiliate membership at any of the churches considering merger
39. Although the UM Book of Discipline requires only a simple majority for the merger to take place, it is strongly recommended that a standard of ⅔ majority be required for passage.
40. There are a number of church planter assessment tools, most notably the resource by Charles Ridley. *A Self-study Manual for Recruiting, Screening, Interviewing and Evaluating Qualified Church Planters.* Fuller Evangelistic Association, 1988.
41. Modified from "High Potential Planter Traits," Path 1, General Board of Discipleship of the UMC, Nashville, TN.

About the Author

DIRK ELLIOTT IS AN ORDAINED MINISTER in the United Methodist Church serving as Director of New Faith Communities and Congregational Development for the Detroit Annual Conference. He holds a M.Div. from Asbury Theological Seminary and has served in ministry for more than thirty years. Dirk is on the Executive Team of Path 1, the church-planting initiative of the United Methodist Church. He coaches, consultants and works with churches and church planters nationwide. For the past ten years, Dirk has been working with churches in the Vital Merger process.

CPSIA information can be obtained at www.ICGtesting.com
Printed in the USA
BVOW04s1804140414

350620BV00003B/8/P